No. 1997
$21.95

469
PASCAL
PROBLEMS

WITH
DETAILED
SOLUTIONS

EUGENE VEKLEROV

TAB BOOKS Inc.
Blue Ridge Summit, PA 17214

FIRST EDITION
FIRST PRINTING

Copyright © 1985 by TAB BOOKS Inc.
Printed in the United States of America

Library of Congress Cataloging in Publication Data

Veklerov, Eugene.
469 Pascal problems with detailed solutions.

Includes index.
1. PASCAL (Computer program language)   I. Title.
II. Title: Four hundred sixty-nine Pascal problems with
detailed solutions.
QA76.73.P2V45   1985   005.13′3   85-17358
ISBN 0-8306-0997-0
ISBN 0-8306-1997-6 (pbk.)

Contents

Acknowledgments

It is a pleasure to record my gratitude to my son Mark Wexler for his competent editing of this book and to my friend Olga Pekelny for her encouraging support.

Introduction

Although only 15 years old, Pascal has firmly established itself in computer science. It is not only becoming the main language of instruction in colleges but is also being used extensively for applications in business and industry. It is now available on dozens of machines ranging from the CRAY-1 to the IBM PC. In brief, Pascal owes this success to the fact that it encourages writing structured programs and employing adequate data structures.

While at present there exists a number of books devoted to Pascal, this book differs from them in its basic philosophy. It consists of a graded series of problems to be solved by the reader. It can be used as a teach-yourself text, as an essential supplement to traditional classroom instruction, or as a reference book. The design of the material is such that the reader will acquire not only knowledge of the intricacies of Pascal programming but also an insight into and taste for good programming in general.

Although existing texts include occasional problems at the end of each chapter, this one features a set of carefully chosen problems arranged in a logical sequence and covering all essential aspects of Pascal programming. The book is divided into two parts. The first part consists of formulations of the problems. To make the text self-contained, each chapter of the first part is preceded by a brief summary of the corresponding theoretical material. These summaries are not intended to replace existing textbooks but only to refresh the memory of the reader who is already familiar with Pascal or to give pointers to the reader with some background in other computer languages. Some finer points of the theoretical material are presented as problems rather than discussed in the summaries.

The levels of difficulty of the problems vary. At one end of the spectrum, there are many rather simple problems aimed at illustrating the syntax of Pascal. These problems are of the type that are given in multiple choice quizzes. Among the more challenging problems are those concerned with file manipulation in Chapter 5, including the problem utilizing the notion of a finite state machine, and the problems introducing Monte Carlo simulation or binary plexes. Sometimes, the simplicity of a problem is deceptive (see problem 5 in the first set of problems in Chapter 1 for example).

Everyone who has taught Pascal knows that there are many alternative organizations of the material, and no one of them is perfect. Thus, it is difficult to proceed to writing meaningful programs before introducing the concept of a file. Logically, however, files belong in the chapter describing other structured types, such as arrays. It does not make much sense to introduce arrays before loops, but studying loops without arrays is rather dry. This list can go on and on. I believe that my arrangement of the chapters is pretty practicable; however, because the book is intended for the reader who studies Pascal on his or her own and can freely move back and forth, I deemed it possible to include several (fewer than ten) problems that use concepts introduced in later chapters.

Chapters 1, 8, 9, and 10 are nontraditional. Chapter 1 presents a brief survey of topics some of which, though not part of the Pascal language, are an integral part of any practical programming. Chapter 8 deals with such diverse issues as style, efficiency, and common errors. It also includes problems that are intended to serve as "food for thought." They are "real life" problems taken from such fields as data processing, simulation, and mathematical statistics that can be used as more challenging projects. Here the reader has a chance to apply the material of this and all preceding chapters. Since, as a rule, there are many solutions to these problems, we provided only very laconic, if any, comments on them.

Two chapters are devoted exclusively to two specific implementations of Pascal. Chapter 9 presents VAX-11 Pascal, which has been developed to run under the VAX/VMS operating system. Chapter 10 presents TURBO Pascal developed by Borland International to run on the IBM PC and compatibles. In conformity with the style of this book, in both of these chapters I zero in on various elements of the language itself rather than on the environment in which the language is used. Solutions to the problems are presented in Chapters 11 through 20.

Part 1
Problems

1 Basic Concepts

The purpose of this chapter is to acquaint you with Pascal. The chapter encompasses many concepts; some of them go beyond the scope of the Pascal language, but they are an integral part of any practical programming. Here is a summary of the most important topics.

An *algorithm* is a sequence of steps leading to the solution of a problem. The development of an algorithm usually precedes writing a program. Algorithms can be described by *flowcharts* or in *pseudocode*.

The flowchart is a pictorial way of representing algorithms. It employs geometric symbols to show various types of actions. Thus, a rectangle usually represents calculations, a rhombus signifies branching, and so on. The symbols are connected by arrows specifying the order of execution. A meaningful description of each action is enclosed within its symbol.

Pseudocode is a more verbal description of an algorithm. Different programmers use different styles of pseudocode, but it is common to utilize some combination of Pascal features and plain English.

There are no universally accepted conventions for flowcharts or pseudocode, and their primary purpose is to be an informal device for outlining a program.

A program in Pascal consists of the following parts:

Program heading
Label declaration part
Constant definition part

Type definition part
Variable declaration part
Procedure and function declaration part
Statement part

Note that Pascal, unlike some other computer languages such as FORTRAN, requires that all variables and labels be explicitly declared. Here is a simple Pascal program that includes a program heading, a constant definition, and a variable declaration (the other parts will be discussed later).

```
PROGRAM CIRCUMFERENCE (INPUT, OUTPUT);
CONST
  PI = 3.14159;
VAR
  RADIUS, CIRCUMFERENCE : REAL;
BEGIN
  WRITELN ('PLEASE ENTER RADIUS');
  READLN (RADIUS);
  CIRCUMFERENCE := 2.0 * PI * RADIUS;
  WRITELN (CIRCUMFERENCE IS ', CIRCUMFERENCE);
END
```

Pascal programs are written in a free format, which means that any number of blanks and carriage returns may occur between any two Pascal symbols (but not within identifiers, numbers, or reserved words). Pascal uses the semicolon to separate statements.

Any sequence of symbols enclosed within braces or curly brackets ({ and }) is a comment. Comments clarify the meaning of a program but do not affect its execution.

Identifiers are the names of variables, constants, types, functions, and procedures. An identifier can be any sequence of letters and digits beginning with a letter. All implementations recognize the first eight characters of identifiers, but some implementations recognize longer identifiers. The following are reserved words which may not be used as identifiers.

AND	END	MOD	REPEAT
ARRAY	FILE	NIL	SET
BEGIN	FOR	NOT	THEN
CASE	FORWARD	OF	TO
CONST	FUNCTION.	OR	TYPE
DIV	GOTO	PACKED	UNTIL
DO	IF	PROCEDURE⁻	VAR
DOWN TO	IN	PROGRAM	WHILE
ELSE	LABEL	RECORD	WITH

Assignment statements have this form:

```
X := Y;
```

where X is the name of a variable and Y is an expression. When the statement is executed, the right-hand-side expression is evaluated, and its value is assigned to the left-hand-side variable.

Pascal has two built-in input procedures; READ and READLN. Both procedures take an arbitrary number of arguments, which are identifiers separated by commas. When a READ or READLN statement is executed, the program searches for the same number of values in the input file and assigns them to the arguments of the procedure. READLN then skips over the rest of the current line in the input file.

The output procedures WRITE and WRITELN are analogous to READ and READLN. Both procedures cause their arguments to be printed, and in addition to that, WRITELN then issues a carriage return.

If an argument of WRITE or WRITELN is a group of characters enclosed between single quotes, the entire group of characters will be printed. To print a single quote itself, two consecutive single quotes must be supplied.

The programmer can control the number of positions reserved for each value. For example, if this statement is executed

```
WRITE (A, B, C:5, D:8:2, E:4);
```

and A is an integer; B, C, and D are reals; and E is a character variable, then A will be printed in the default field, which is implementation dependent. B and C will be printed in floating point notation in the default field and in five columns. D will be printed in decimal notation in eight columns with two columns reserved for the digits of D lying after the decimal point. Four columns will be reserved for E. All values will be right-justified, but if they do not fit in the number of places allowed, the printer will use as many places as necessary.

ALGORITHMS AND PROGRAMS

1. You are going to a party. The host has given you directions or an algorithm describing how to get there. The directions read in part

   Take highway 101 north.
   Drive 5 miles.
   Take the exit marked "Main Street."

   What is the flaw in this algorithm?

2. There are three memory locations X, Y, and Z, containing the numbers $<X>$, $<Y>$, and $<Z>$. Write an algorithm for finding and printing the largest number.

3. Let X, Y, and Z be three memory locations and $<X>$, $<Y>$, and $<Z>$ their contents. Describe the contents of X, Y, and Z after execution of the following algorithm.

   ```
   - If < Y > is less than < X >
          then swap < X > and < Y >
   ```

```
                    else do nothing;
    - If < Z > is less than < Y >
            then swap < Y > and < Z >
            else do nothing;
    - If < Y > is less than < X >
            then swap < X > and < Y >
            else do nothing.
```

Why is there a need for step 3 which is the same as step 1?

4. There are three unknown letters in memory locations X, Y, and Z. Write an algorithm that will print 0 if all letters are different and 1 if at least two of them are the same.

5. Design an algorithm that will swap the contents of two memory locations. Try not to use a temporary memory location.

6. An editor is a means for (choose the right answer)

   a. Creating and modifying a file
   b. Debugging a program
   c. Compiling a program from Pascal into machine language
   d. Directing the computer to perform given operations

7. A compiler is

   a. The machine language version of a Pascal program
   b. A program that converts a Pascal program into the object code
   c. A set of software provided by the manufacturer
   d. A set of machine language instructions

8. An operating system is

   a. An editor
   b. A language that allows the user to communicate with the computer
   c. A set of programs that control the overall operation of the computer to provide an efficient use of its resources
   d. A set of programs written in a low level language

9. Interactive programs are those which

   a. Have a higher priority than all other programs
   b. Solicit some data from the user and provide the user with some information
   c. Are submitted to the computer from the terminal
   d. Are written according to the rules of structured programming

10. A student wrote a program and made the following errors:

    a. Typed two plus signs in a row instead of one (e.g., A + + B)
    b. Replaced a plus sign with a minus sign
    c. Omitted a closing parenthesis in a READ statement
    d. Misspelled the word WRITE as RITE
    e. Misspelled a variable name in an assignment statement
    f. Tried to compute $LN(-3.14)$
    g. Forgot to declare a variable
    h. Misspelled a word in a comment
    i. Tried to find the square root of -4

Which of the above are compile-time errors, which are run-time errors and which are neither?

11. You are allowed to insert any number of blanks and carriage returns

    a. Within an identifier
    b. Between a plus sign and the next operand
    c. Between the word PROGRAM and the following left parenthesis

Which of the foregoing statements are correct?

MAJOR PARTS OF A PASCAL PROGRAM

1. Must every program have

    a. A program heading?
    b. Comments?
    c. A constant definition part?
    d. A label definition part?
    e. A variable declaration part?
    f. A statement part?

2. Write a simple program that does not have a variable declaration part.

3. A student misspelled the program name in the program heading. Describe the effect of that error.

4. A comment takes more than one line. Is it necessary to enclose each line between curly brackets?

5. In some situations a good way of deleting a program segment is simply commenting it, i.e., enclosing it in curly brackets. Suppose that the program segment itself contains comments, so that we can talk about nested comments such as in this example:

{THIS IS AN EXAMPLE OF NESTED COMMENTS {EXAMPLE} BUT WILL IT WORK?}

Will it work?

6. A student wanted to use two comments separated with several statements as follows:

```
{ ... }
. . . . . . . .
. . . . . . . .
. . . . . . . ;
{ ... }
```

but forgot to type the closing brace after the first comment. What will happen?

7. Some character sets do not include braces or curly brackets ({ and }). If so, what characters are used to delimit comments?

8. Which of the comments below are placed legally?

```
a. AREA := L{LENGTH} * W{WIDTH}
b. AR{THIS IS A KNOWN FORMULA}
   EA := L * W
c. AREA :{EQUALS}= L * W
d. PI := 3.{SEE NEXT LINE}
   14
```

9. Which of the following may be used as labels?

   a. Characters
   b. Strings
   c. Integer numbers
   d. Real numbers
   e. Unsigned integer numbers

10. A student wrote a program that needed exactly three labels. Which of the following is an error?

   a. The student chose these labels: 100, 200, and 250.
   b. The label 200 appeared in the statement part before the label 100.
   c. The label 250 was used with several statements.

11. Which of the following constants are predefined in Pascal?

a. Maximum integer number
b. Minimum integer number
c. Maximum real number
d. Minimum real number
e. Minimum positive real number
f. Maximum negative real number

12. A programmer is going to use a constant denoting the sales tax. Which of these identifiers would you prefer?

a. X
b. ST
c. SALESTAX

13. Is this constant definition valid?

```
CONST
    NAME = 'JOHN SMITH';
```

14. Which of these three constant definitions is/are invalid? (D is a variable initialized with a READ statement).

```
CONST
    A = 0.25;
    B = -A;
    C = D;
```

15. Are the following constant definitions valid?

```
CONST
    PI = 2.7983;
    E = 3.1415;
```

16. Rewrite the following program using a constant and explain advantages of the new version.

```
PROGRAM CIRCLE (INPUT,OUTPUT);
VAR
    RADIUS, AREA, CIRCUMFERENCE : REAL;
BEGIN
    WRITELN('PLEASE, ENTER RADIUS');
    READLN(RADIUS);
    AREA := 3.14 * RADIUS * RADIUS;
    CIRCUMFERENCE := 2.0 * 3.14 * RADIUS;
```

```
            WRITELN('AREA IS ',AREA,'CIRCUMFERENCE IS
',CIRCUMFERENCE)
        END.
```

17. What is the difference between the effect of the declaration

```
VAR
    A : REAL;
    B : REAL;
```

and

```
VAR
    A, B : REAL;
```

18. To initialize a variable is to

a. Declare it
b. Assign a starting value to it
c. Use it in the statement part of the program
d. Use it as the left hand side variable of an assignment statement

19. What is the value of a variable before its initialization?

20. Find the error in this program.

```
PROGRAM SIMPLE(OUTPUT);
VAR
    X,Y,Z : INTEGER;
BEGIN
    X := 0;
    Z := X + Y;
    WRITELN(Z)
END;
```

IDENTIFIERS AND ASSIGNMENTS

1. Which of the following identifiers are valid and which are not?

a. N
b. MYINCOMETAX
c. My Income Tax
d. MY INCOME TAX
e. PRINT85
f. M&M
g. RECORD
h. A B

i. 85PRINT
j. AAAAAAAAAAAAAAAAAA
k. MY_INCOME_TAX
l. MY*INCOME*TAX
m. 85
n. CaliforniaStateUniversity
o. SET1

2. What will happen if these identifiers

   MYINCOMETAXIN1984
   MYINCOMETAXIN1985
   MYINCOMETAXIN1986

   are used within a program?

3. NAME has been declared as a character variable. Is this statement valid?

   NAME := 'JOHN SMITH'

4. Is it legal to introduce two different variables named A with this declaration?

   ```
   VAR
      A : REAL;
      A : INTEGER;
   ```

5. May EXP be a variable name?

6. Which of the following assignment statements are valid and which are not?

   a. **X = Y + Z**   d. **X := X**
   b. **X : = X + 1**   e. **X + Y := Z**
   c. **X := X + 1**   f. **X := Y / ZERO**

7. The values of A, B, and C are 1, 2, and 3, respectively. What will the values be after the following assignment statements are executed?

   ```
   A := B;
   B := C;
   C := A
   ```

   Will the results be the same if the assignment statements are executed in a different sequence, for example

   ```
   B := C;
   C := A;
   A := B
   ```

8. Explain the difference between these assignment statements.

   a. Between **A := B** and **A := 'B'**
   b. Between **A := 7** and **A := '7'**

9. A is a character variable. Is there any difference between these two assignment statements?

a. **A := ' '**

and

b. **A := ''**

(A blank between the single quotes in the former statement and no character in the latter).

10. A is an integer variable. Is there any difference between these two assignment statements?

   a. **A := 0;**
   and

   b. **A := ;**

11. Can this

   A := B = C

   be a valid Pascal statement?

12. A student inadvertently typed several semicolons in a row after an assignment statement. What will be the effect of this mistake?

INPUT AND OUTPUT FEATURES

1. Write a program that will print a square. Use minus signs to draw the horizontal sides and exclamation marks to draw the vertical sides.

2. Write a program that will print your name using asterisks; for example:

```
* * * * * *     *          *      * * * * *    * * * * * *    *          *    * * * * * *
*               *          *     *             *              * *        *    *
*               *          *     *             *              *  *       *    *
* * * * *        *          *     * * * * *     * * * * *      *   *      *    * * * * *
*               *          *     *      *      *              *    *     *    *
*               *      *   *     *       *     *              *     * *  *    *
* * * * * *         * * *        * * * *       * * * * * *     *          *    * * * * * *
```

3. Write a program that will prompt the user to enter a three letter word at the keyboard and then print the same word backwards.

4. What will be printed after execution of this statement?

   ```
   WRITELN ('''')
   ```

5. Describe the difference between the output produced by this program segment

```
WRITE('*');
WRITE('*');
WRITE('*');
WRITELN
```

and this one

```
WRITELN('*');
WRITELN('*');
WRITELN('*')
```

6. Describe the effect of this program segment in a batch environment.

```
READLN;
READLN;
READLN
```

7. X is an integer variable and Y is a character variable. Will the statement

```
READLN(X,Y)
```

produce different results if the input line is

    5   C

or

    5C

8. Variables A and B have been declared as integer variables and C as a real variable. Describe the effect of the statement

```
READLN(A,B,C)
```

if the input is:

a.	41	7	− 3.7		
b.	41		7		− 3.7
c. (on 2 lines		41)			7
			− 3.7		
d.	41	7	− 3.7	50	
e.	41	7			
f.	417	− 3.7			
g.	41.0	7	− 3.7		
h	A	7	− 3.7		

9. A programmer wanted to type

11

```
READ(A,B)
```

but made an error and typed

a. `READ(A B)`
b. `READ(AB)`
c. `READ(B,A)`

Describe the effect of each error.

10. X, Y, and Z are integer variables and $<X>$, $<Y>$, and $<Z>$ are their values. Write Pascal statements that will produce the output in this form:

```
        X           !           Y           !           Z
                    !                       !
--------------------------------------------------------------
                    !                       !
        < X >       !       < Y >           !       < Z >
```

Use minus signs and exclamation marks to draw horizontal and vertical lines.

11. X, Y, and Z are integer variables equal to 17, 5 and 1967, respectively. Depict the output produced by these statements:

a. `WRITELN(X,Y,Z)`
b. `WRITELN('X =',X,'Y =',Y,'Z =',Z)`
c. `WRITELN('X =',X:2,' Y =',Y:1,' Z =',Z:4)`
d. `WRITELN('X =',X:3,',  Y =',Y:2,',  Z =',Z:5)`

12. X, Y, and Z are equal to 1, 11, and 111, respectively. Write a program that will print these values as a

a. right justified column.
b. left justified column.

13. Write a shorter statement that will achieve the same effect as

```
WRITE ('          ')
```

(10 blanks between the single quotes).

14. What will be the output produced by the statements

a. `WRITELN (X : 6 : 2)`
b. `WRITELN (X : 10 : 2)`
c. `WRITELN (X : 5 : 2)`

d. **WRITELN (X : 6 : 1)**
e. **WRITELN (X : 8 : 4)**

if X is 123.48?

15. Is the statement

   WRITELN (X : Y + Z : Y - Z)

   valid if X is a real and Y and Z are integers? If it is, what will be the output produced by it if X is 3.14, Y is 5 and Z is 4?

16. You want to have two tables printed on separate pages. Each table is 15 lines long. To have the second table printed on the new page, you may use several WRITELN statements with no arguments. There is a more convenient way to achieve the same effect. What is it?

17. A programmer wanted to type this statement

   WRITE('ABC',DEF,'GHI',JKL)

   but inadvertently omitted the second single quote. What will happen as a result of this error?

2 Expressions

Every variable in Pascal has a *type* which must be explicitly declared. A type describes the set of values that can be assigned to a variable. While some types are defined by the programmer, basic types are predefined.

Pascal predefines four standard scalar data types: *integer, character, Boolean,* and *real.* The first three types are referred to as ordinal types (because their orderings are analogous to that of integers).

The integer data type denotes integer values, both positive and negative. The CHARacter data type denotes single character values, such as A, S, +, %, and 4. The Boolean data type consists of two values, TRUE and FALSE. The real data type comprises real number values. Real constants can be written either in the conventional decimal or floating point notation. In floating point notation − 3.14E5, for example, means that − 3.14 is to be multiplied by 10 raised to the fifth power.

The following arithmetic operators may be used with real operands and produce real results: + (addition), − (subtraction), * (multiplication), and / (division). The following arithmetic operators may be used with integer operands and produce integer results: +, −, *, DIV (integer division), and MOD (modulus). Just as in mathematics, if an expression includes several operators, additions and subtractions are performed after all other operators. Otherwise, an expression is evaluated from left to right unless some parts of it are enclosed in parentheses. Both operands of an integer operator must be integers. The operands of a real operator may be either real or integer.

Pascal provides a number of operators that can be used to construct Boolean expressions. First, there are six relational operators

$<$ less than
$<=$ less than or equal to
$>$ greater than
$>=$ greater than or equal to
$=$ equal to
$<>$ not equal to

that yield the value TRUE if the relationship between the two operands is in correct order and FALSE otherwise. Second, Boolean expressions can be constructed with the logical operators AND, OR, and NOT. The order of precedence of both arithmetic and Boolean operators is given in the following table in the order of decreasing precedence (all operators in the same line have equal precedence).

NOT
*, /, DIV, MOD, AND
+, −, OR
relational operators

Expressions that contain several operators of equal precedence are evaluated from left to right, but as usual, the presence of parentheses overrides the order of operators.
    Pascal has the predefined functions shown in Table 2-1.

TYPES

1. Which of the following are valid integer constants?

   a. **75**
   b. **−231**
   c. **28.**
   d. **3,000,000**
   e. **45 000**

   f. **+0026**
   g. **34.0**
   h. **−00**
   i. **MAXINT**

2. Which of the following are valid real constants?

   a. **+3.14**
   b. **−3.14**
   c. **12.**
   d. **.003**
   e. **47**

   f. **47.0**
   g. **26,75**
   h. **−.75**
   i. **−00.000**

3. Which of the following are valid real constants?

   a. **3.7E5**
   b. **3.7E−5**
   c. **3.7E5**

   d. **3.7E12**
   e. **3.7E4.5**
   f. **−3.7E−7**

g. 5E2   i. 3.14E0
h. 3.14E1   j. 3.14E-0

4. Convert the following constants to floating point form.

a. 5000.0   c. 0.0000063
b. -4375.0   d. -1.1

Table 2-1. The Predefined Functions in Pascal.

Name	Description of Function	Argument Type	Result Type
ABS	absolute value	integer or real	same as argument
SQR	square	integer or real	same as argument
SQRT	square root	integer or real	real
EXP	exponentiation	integer or real	real
LN	natural logarithm	integer or real	real
SIN	sine	integer or real	real
COS	cosine	integer or real	real
ARCTAN	arctangent	integer or real	real
ROUND	rounding	real	integer
TRUNC	truncation	real	integer
SUCC	successor	any ordinal	same as argument
PRED	predecessor	any ordinal	same as argument
ORD	ordinal value	any ordinal	integer
CHR	character value of given ordinal value	integer	character
ODD	TRUE if argument is odd	integer	Boolean
EOLN	TRUE if end of line is encountered	file	Boolean
EOF	TRUE if end of file is encountered	file	Boolean

5. Convert the following constants to decimal form.

   a. -4.7E+3   c. 4.7E3
   b. -4.7E-3   d. 4.7E-3

6. Which of the following expressions are valid?

   a. 10E7 * 4.1   e. 14 DIV 7 * 3.0
   b. 7 DIV 2   f. 3.0 * 14 DIV 7
   c. 2.7 - 5   g. 4.105E(4 - 2)
   d. 6.6 DIV 3   h. (4.105 + 2.73)E3

7. AR and BR are real variables and CI and DI are integers. Which of the following assignment statements are valid?

   a. AR := CI   f. AR := CI / DI
   b. CI := AR   g. AR := CI DIV DI / BR
   c. AR := BR + CI   h. AR := CI / DI DIV BR
   d. CI := BR + DI   i. AR := CI * DI * BR
   e. AR := CI DIV DI   j. CI := DI + 1.0

8. ACH is a character variable. Which of the following assignment statements are valid?

   a. ACH := B   f. ACH := ACH
   b. ACH := 7   g. ACH := - ACH
   c. ACH := '7'   h. ACH := '-7'
   d. ACH := ' '   i. ACH := -'7'
   e. ACH := 'BCD'   j. ACH := 'B' + 'C'

ARITHMETIC AND BOOLEAN OPERATORS

1. Evaluate the following expressions.

   a. 3 * ((4 - 1) * 2)
   b. (7 - 2) DIV (4 + 6 DIV 2)
   c. 16 DIV 2 / 2

2. Insert parentheses in the following expressions that will clarify them but will not change their values.

   a. 17 - 4 * 3 DIV 7
   b. 4.6 * 3 - 8 / 2
   c. A DIV A DIV A * B

3. Remove unneeded parentheses.

17

a. `(A - 3.4) - ((7 * NUMBER) + 4)`
b. `-((B - C) * 6.0)`

4. Is – A MOD B evaluated as (– A) MOD B or as – (A MOD B)?

5. Evaluate the following expressions.

a. `5 MOD (-2)`   c. `(-5) MOD 2`
b. `5 MOD 0`   d. `(-5) MOD (-2)`

6. What is the value of

a. `(-5) DIV 2`   c. `(-5) DIV (-2)`
b. `5 DIV (-2)`   d. `0 DIV (-2)`

7. What will happen if the program segment below is executed?

```
A := MAXINT;
B := 2 * A
```

8. Combine these assignment statements

```
NUMBER := 2 * NUMBER;
NUMBER := 4 - NUMBER;
NUMBER := 7 * NUMBER
```

into one statement.

9. Some computer languages have exponentiation operators. How about Pascal?

10. MINUTE is an integer variable denoting a time interval in minutes. Write expressions yielding the same time interval in

a. hours
b. days
c. weeks

as integer values.

11. MYSTERY is a five digit integer number. Let its digits, from left to right, be a, b, c, d, and e. Provide expressions yielding integer numbers whose digits, from left to right, are

a. e, d, c, b and a.
b. c, d, e, a and b.

12. Which of the following Boolean expressions are valid?

a. **3 > 4 AND 7 = 5**
b. **4 < 5 < 6**
c. **3 < = 4**
d. **2 > 10**
e. **TRUE AND FALSE**
f. **TRUE OR NOT (7 − 3 <= 4)**
g. **A AND NOT OR B**
h. **2 + 5 = 7 * 3**
i. **TRUE OR TRUE**

13. A1, A2, and A3 are Boolean variables equal to TRUE, FALSE and FALSE, respectively. Evaluate the following expressions.

a. **NOT A1 AND NOT A2**
b. **A1 OR A2 AND A3**
c. **(NOT A1 OR A2) AND (A2 OR A3)**
d. **FALSE OR NOT A1 AND A2 OR NOT A3**

14. Insert parentheses to make the following Boolean expressions clearer.

a. **A OR B OR NOT C AND D**
b. **NOT (3 > X) AND (7 <> Y) OR (X = Y)**

15. Remove unneeded parentheses.

a. **((NOT A) AND (NOT B)) OR C**
b. **((NOT A) OR (NOT B)) AND C**

16. Is the statement

    WRITE (3 > 4)

valid and, if so, what will be printed?

17. X is a Boolean variable. May it be used in the statement

    READ (X)

18. The expression (3 > 5) AND X always equals FALSE, regardless of the value of X. Suppose that X itself is an expression which happens to be invalid. Then, will the entire expression equal FALSE, or will it be invalid?

19. B is a Boolean variable. What is its value after execution of these statements?

a. **B := 'LOVE' <> 'WORK'**
b. **B := 'MARK' > 'OLGA'**
c. **B := 'MARK' > 'MARY'**
d. **B := 'MARK' > 'EUGENE'**

STANDARD FUNCTIONS

1. Evaluate the following expressions. Include a decimal point if a result is real.

   a. SQR (2)
   b. SQR (2.25 – SQR (2.5))
   c. SQRT (SQR (3) + SQR (4))
   d. COS (0)
   e. SIN (0)
   f. SIN (90)
   g. LN (1)
   h. EXP (0)
   i. ORD ('D') – ORD ('B')
   j. CHR (37)
   k. CHR (ORD ('K') + 2)
   l. ODD (X), where X is 9
   m. ABS (ABS (–2))
   n. SQRT (ABS (–4))
   o. TRUNC (–99.9)
   p. –ROUND (9.8)
   q. ARCTAN (1)
   r. SUCC (PRED (PRED ('C')))

2. Convert the following mathematical expressions to Pascal expressions.

   a. $\dfrac{x + y + z}{\sqrt{x^2 + y^2 + z^2}}$

   b. $(abc)^2$

   c. $\ln\left(1 + \left|\dfrac{a+b}{a-b}\right|\right)$

   d. $2 \sin\left(\dfrac{x+y}{2}\right)\cos\left(\dfrac{x-y}{2}\right)$

3. Use a pocket calculator to evaluate these expressions.

   a. SQRT (SIN (0.453))
   b. EXP (SQR (2.5) – SQR (1.5))
   c. ARCTAN (2.3 / 0.457)

4. Does TRUNC (X + Y) always equal TRUNC (X) + TRUNC (Y)?

5. Does ROUND (X + Y) always equal ROUND (X) + ROUND (Y)?

6. Explain the difference between ORD (A) and ORD ('A').

7. Is COS a reserved word in Pascal? May you define a function called COS as follows?

```
FUNCTION COS (X : REAL) : REAL;
BEGIN
    COS := X / 2.0
END;
```

8. Write a Pascal expression that will return the Boolean value TRUE if the value

of the integer variable NUMBER is even and FALSE otherwise.

9. A student said that TRUNC (3.7) is 3.0. Was the student correct?

10. Look up the values of

   a. ORD ('A')   c. CHR (54)
   b. ORD ('=')   d. CHR (106)

   if your implementation uses the ASCII character set.

11. Are the expressions ORD (19) and ORD (−71) valid?

12. Let us assume that the last character of a character set is a semicolon. What is the value of SUCC (';')?

13. X is a real variable. Write a Pascal expression that will

   a. round X to the nearest hundredth
   b. truncate all decimal places beginning with the thousandth, that is, 293.0784 should become 293.07

14. X is a real variable. Write a Pascal expression that will

   a. round X to the nearest hundred
   b. replace all digits of X beginning with the tens place with zeros, that is, 293.0784 should become 200.0.

15. Is it true that SUCC ('5') is '6'?

16. Describe what this expression

   $$(X + ABS (X)) / 2.0$$

   will yield, where X may take on any real value.

17. Write Pascal expressions equivalent to the following mathematical expressions.

   a. x^3 c. $x^{1.35}$
   b. $\sqrt[5]{x}$ d. $\log_2 x$

18. Write Pascal expressions that will yield these trigonometric functions.

   a. tan x   d. csc x   g. arccot x
   b. cot x   e. arcsin x   h. arcsec x
   c. sec x   f. arccos x   i. arccsc x

3　Control Statements

If a program consisted only of assignment statements and input and output procedures, the statements would be executed in succession and each statement would be executed once and only once. Pascal provides a number of control statements that can change the order in which statements are executed, thereby making programs more flexible. These statements are IF, CASE, FOR, WHILE, REPEAT, and GOTO.

The IF statement has two forms:

```
IF <Boolean expression>
   THEN <statement 1>
   ELSE <statement 2>
```
or
```
IF <Boolean expression>
   THEN <statement 1>
```

If the Boolean expression equals TRUE, statement 1 is executed. Otherwise, statement 2 or any empty statement is executed, depending on which form of the IF statement is used. If it is necessary to perform several actions when the Boolean expression is TRUE and/or FALSE, compound statements can be used. A compound statement is a group of statements enclosed between the *statement brackets*, BEGIN and END. Here is an example of the use of compound statements.

```
IF AGE > 59.5
    THEN BEGIN
            A := 3;
            B := 4
        END
    ELSE BEGIN
            A := 2
            B := 3
        END
```

The CASE statement is a generalization of the IF statement. It has the form

```
CASE <expression> OF
    <value 1> : <statement 1> ;
    <value 2> : <statement 2> ;
                . . .
    <value n> : <statement n>
END;
```

The CASE expression must be of a scalar ordinal type. The list of values is called the constant list. Each constant is followed by a statement (which may be an empty statement).

If the value of the expression belongs to the constant list, the statement immediately following the value is executed. If the value is not listed, the result is implementation dependent (some versions of Pascal will continue on to the next statement, while others will consider this a run time error). Several constants may be combined if they call for the same action; for example:

```
CASE X OF
    1, 3, 5 : WRITELN '(SMALL ODD NUMBER)';
    2, 4    : WRITELN '(SMALL EVEN NUMBER)';
    6       : ;
    7, 8, 9 : WRITELN '(SMALL ODD NUMBER)';
END
```

There are 3 iterative constructions or loop statements in Pascal: FOR, REPEAT, and WHILE. The FOR statement has 2 forms:

```
FOR <counter> := <initial value> TO <final value>
DO <statement>
```

or

```
FOR <counter> := <initial value> DOWNTO <final value>
DO <statement>
```

The statement (it can be a compound statement) is executed once for every value of the counter variable, which takes all values between the initial value and the final value inclusive. The counter variable and the initial and final values must have the same ordinal type and may not be altered within the loop. The initial and final values can be expressions. If, in the case of TO (DOWNTO), the initial value is greater (less) than the final value, the statement is not executed at all, which is not the case in other computer languages.

The other two iterative constructions have these forms:

```
      WHILE <Boolean expression>
      DO <statement>
and
      REPEAT
        <statement 1>;
        <statement 2>;
           . . .
      UNTIL <Boolean expression>
```

In the case of the WHILE statement, the Boolean expression is evaluated before each iteration, and as long as it equals TRUE, the statement is executed. In the case of the REPEAT statement, all statements are executed, then the Boolean expression is evaluated, and if it equals FALSE, all statements are executed again, and so on. In other words, all statements are executed at least once. The WHILE loop will terminate as soon as the Boolean expression is FALSE, whereas the REPEAT loop will terminate as soon as it is TRUE.

The GOTO statement, or the unconditional transfer of control has the form

```
      GOTO <label>
```

and it simply causes control to be transferred to the statement with the given label. There are some restrictions on where in the program the label may appear. For example, control may not be transferred to the middle of an iterative structure (FOR, REPEAT, WHILE) or of a conditional structure (IF, CASE) from the outside of such a structure.

Finally, it would not be difficult to replace CASE, FOR, and other control statements with constructions using IF and GOTO statements, but these constructions would be messy. Generally, the excessive use of GOTO statements leads to tangled structures and should be avoided.

THE IF STATEMENT

1. What is the output of this program segment?

```
      IF ODD(10)
        THEN WRITELN ('10 IS ODD')
        ELSE BEGIN
```

```
            WRITELN ('10 IS EVEN');
            WRITELN ('AND DON''T FORGET THAT ODD
                     RETURNS BOOLEAN VALUES')
      END
```

2. What is the output of this program segment?

```
   IF (2 * 2 = 5) < (2 * 2 = 4)
      THEN WRITELN('TRUE IS GREATER THAN FALSE')
      ELSE WRITELN('FALSE IS GREATER THAN TRUE')
```

3. Combine the two IF statements into one.

```
   IF A < B
      THEN X := 1
      ELSE X := 2;
   IF A < B
      THEN READ (Y)
      ELSE READ (Z)
```

4. Combine the two IF statements into one.

```
   IF A <> B
      THEN I := J
      ELSE I := -J;
   IF MYINCOME >= YOURINCOME
      THEN I := J
      ELSE I := -J
```

5. Combine the two IF statements into one.

```
   IF RATE > 0
      THEN IF RATE < 1
              THEN A := 0
              ELSE A := 1
      ELSE A := 1
```

6. Explain the difference between construction A and construction B. What will happen if BEGIN and END are omitted?

```
   a. IF A < B
         THEN BEGIN
                 IF C = D
                    THEN X := Y
              END
         ELSE U := W
```

```
b. IF A < B
       THEN BEGIN
                 IF C = D
                    THEN X := Y
                    ELSE U := W
          END
```

7. Write a program that will prompt the user to enter the coefficients of a linear equation and solve it.

8. Write a program that will prompt the user to enter the coefficients of a quadratic equation and solve it.

9. Write a program segment that will prompt the user to enter an integer number between 1 and 100 and verify that the entry is in that range. If the number indeed lies between 1 and 100, it is processed by another program segment, which is irrelevant to this problem. In case it does not, consider several options:
   a . A warning is given but the number is processed by the other segment anyway.
   b . An appropriate message is given and the program stops.
   c . The user is given another chance to enter a valid number. If the second attempt fails too, either option A or option B follows.
   . The user is given 2 other attempts to enter a valid number. If all of them fail, either option A or option B follows.
   e . The user is prompted to enter a number until it is valid. There is no restriction on the number of attempts.

10. What will be the value of A after this program segment is executed?

```
A := 0;
IF A >= 7
   THEN; BEGIN
            A := 1;
            WRITELN ('WATCH OUT')
         END
```

THE CASE STATEMENT

1. What will the value of Y be after the following program segment is executed?

```
X := 5
CASE X OF
    1    : Y := 3;
    2, 3 : Y := 1;
    4    : Y := 7;
    5    : Y := 2
END;
```

2. What will be printed by this program segment?

```
SUM := 0.0
FOR COUNTER := 7 downto 4
DO    CASE COUNTER OF
          1, 4, 7 : SUM := SUM + 1;
          2, 3, 6 : ;
          0, 1, 5 : SUM := SUM + 2
      END;
WRITELN('SUM = ',SUM);
```

Find the error in each of the following program segments (3 - 9).

3.
```
CASE SQR(X) + SQR(Y) OF
    1, 4 : Z := X - Y;
    0, 5 : Z := X + Y;
    4    : Z := X;
    9    : Z := Y
END;
```

4.
```
FOR I := 5 TO 10
DO    CASE I OF
          1, 2, 3, 4 : LETTER := 'A';
          5, 7, 9    : LETTER := 'B';
          6, 8       : LETTER := 'C'
      END;
```

5.
```
CASE A + B OF
    2      : X := 0;
    3, 4.5 : X := 1
END;
```

6.
```
CASE 3 * A OF
    X : N := 1.4;
    Y : N := 1.7
END;
```

7.
```
CASE 3 * A OF
    'X' : N := 1.4;
    'Y' : N := 1.7
END;
```

8.
```
CASE X + 4.0 OF
   '1'   : A := B;
   '2'   : A := -B
END;
```

9.
```
CASE X OF
   10 : K := K - 1
   20 :
END;
```

10. A programmer replaced the following statement

```
CASE A OF
   'X' : WRITELN('A = X');
   'Y' : WRITELN('A = Y');
   'Z' : WRITELN('A = Z')
END;
```

in a program with this CASE statement

```
CASE A OF
   'Y' : WRITELN('A = Y');
   'X' : WRITELN('A = X');
   'Z' : WRITELN('A = Z')
END;
```

Could the program run differently because of this change?

11. What constant list should appear in the CASE statement if the CASE expression is SQR(N) MOD 3?

12. Write a program that will print out the months of the year. The user enters a number and the program displays the corresponding month.

13. Rewrite the following program segment using a CASE statement. Assume that K has been declared as an integer variable.

```
IF (K <= 10) AND (K > 0) THEN
   IF K > 5 THEN
      IF K < 8 THEN
         X := 0
      ELSE
         X := 1
```

```
            ELSE
               IF  K  >  2  THEN
                     X  :=  3
               ELSE
                     X  :=  4;
```

14. Motorists buying gasoline at full service pumps pay $1.50, $1.35, or $1.18 for a gallon of premium, unleaded, or regular gasoline, respectively. Motorists using mini-service or self-service pumps get 5 percent or 10 percent discounts, respectively. Write a program segment that will compute the cost of a purchase if the user enters the amount and the grade of gasoline and the type of service.

15. Explain what the following program does.

```
PROGRAM GRADES (INPUT,OUTPUT);
VAR
    SCORE, A, B, C, D, F : INTEGER;
BEGIN
    A := 0;
    B := 0;
    C := 0;
    D := 0;
    F := 0;
    REPEAT
       WRITELN('PLEASE, ENTER SCORE');
       READLN(SCORE);
       IF (SCORE <= 10) AND (SCORE >= 0) THEN
          CASE SCORE OF
             0, 1, 2, 3 : F := F + 1;
                      4 : D := D + 1;
                   5, 6 : C := C + 1;
                   7, 8 : B := B + 1;
                  9, 10 : A := A + 1
          END
       ELSE
          WRITELN('INVALID SCORE');
    UNTIL SCORE < 0;
    WRITELN('A          B          C          D     F');
    WRITELN(A,B,C,D,F);
END.
```

16. A brokerage firm charges commissions according to this schedule.

Dollar Range Per Transaction	Commission Rates
$ 0 - 2,999	$18 + 1.2% of principal amount
$3,000 - 5,999	$36 + .6% of principal amount
$6,000 - 10,000	$57 + .3% of principal amount

Write a program segment that will compute and print the commission for any transaction under $10,000.

17. Write a calculator program. The user enters two real numbers followed by +, −, * or /. The program computes and prints the sum, the difference, the product, or the quotient of the two numbers, respectively.

18. Write a program that, given the date of birth, will compute the day of the week on which any student in your class was born.

LOOPS

1. Write a program that will compute

   a. the sum of all integers from 1 to 100;
   b. the sum of all even integers from 1 to 100;
   c. the sum of all odd integers from 1 to 100.

2. Write a program that will compute

   a. the sum of all integers from 1 to 100 divisible by both 3 and 4;
   b. the sum of all integers from 1 to 100 not divisible by either 3 or 4.

3. Write a program that will prompt the user to enter a series of numbers and compute their mean and standard deviation. To mark the end of the series, the user must type a certain sentinel number, say −100.

4. Write a program that will find the first 10 numbers that, when divided by 2, 3, and 5, leave a remainder of 1.

5. Write a program that will determine whether any given integer greater than 2 is prime or composite.

6. Write a program that will prompt the user to enter a series of numbers and compute how many positive and negative numbers will have been entered. To mark the end of the series, the user must type a sentinel number, say −100.

7. Write a program segment that will compute the sum of all numbers in the following table.

$$\begin{array}{ccccc}
1 & 2 & 3 & \ldots & 10 \\
2 & 4 & 6 & \ldots & 20 \\
3 & 6 & 9 & \ldots & 30 \\
\hline
10 & 20 & 30 & \ldots & 100
\end{array}$$

8. Modify the previous problem so that the program will compute the sum of all numbers in the table lying above the diagonal connecting the upper-left and lower-right corners.

9. Write a program that will use the trapezoid rule to compute $\int_{a}^{b} e^{-x^2}\, dx.$ The trapezoid rule may be described as follows. The interval [a, b] is divided into n equal subintervals $[x_{i\text{-}1}, x_i]$, where $x_i = a + ih$. We then approximate the value of $\int_{x_{i-1}}^{x_i} \#6\, f(x)dx$ by the area of the trapezoid having vertices $(x_{i-1}, 0)$, (x_{i-1}, y_{i-1}), and $(x_i, 0)$, where $y_i = f(x_i)$. The approximation for the entire interval is the sum of the areas of these trapezoids.

10. Describe the output produced by each of the following program segments.

a.
```
I := 0;
REPEAT
    WRITELN ('HELLO');
    I := I + 1
UNTIL I = 5
```

b.
```
I := 0;
REPEAT
    WRITELN ('HELLO')
UNTIL I = 5
```

c.
```
I := 0;
REPEAT
    WRITELN ('HELLO');
    I := I - 1
UNTIL I = 5
```

d.
```
I := 0;
REPEAT
    WRITELN ('HELLO');
    I := I + 2
UNTIL I = 5
```

Find the error in each of the following programs (11 - 16).

11.

```
PROGRAM ERROR1 (OUTPUT);
VAR
    INITIALVALUE, FINALVALUE : INTEGER;
BEGIN
        INITIALVALUE := -6;
        FINALVALUE := -2;
```

```
            FOR I := INITIALVALUE TO FINALVALUE
            DO WRITELN ('HELLO')
      END.


12.   PROGRAM ERROR2 (OUTPUT);
      VAR
          COUNTER : CHAR;
      BEGIN
            FOR COUNTER := 'Z' DOWNTO 'U'
            DO BEGIN
                    WRITELN ('HELLO');
                    COUNTER := PRED (COUNTER)
                END
      END.


13.   PROGRAM ERROR3 (OUTPUT);
      VAR
          INITIALVALUE, FINALVALUE, COUNTER : INTEGER;
      BEGIN
            INITIALVALUE := -5;
            FINALVALUE := 5;
            FOR COUNTER := INITIALVALUE TO FINALVALUE
            DO BEGIN
                    WRITELN ('HELLO');
                    FINALVALUE := FINALVALUE - 1
                END
      END.

14.   PROGRAM ERROR4 (OUTPUT);
      VAR
          I : INTEGER;
      BEGIN
            FOR I := 1 DOWNTO 100 / 3
            DO WRITELN (I)
      END.

15.   PROGRAM ERROR5 (OUTPUT);
      VAR
          I : INTEGER;
      BEGIN
            FOR I := 'D' TO 'H'
            DO WRITELN ('HELLO')
      END.
```

16.
```
    PROGRAM ERROR6 (OUTPUT);
    VAR
        A, B : INTEGER;
    BEGIN
            FOR A + B := 1 TO 10
            DO WRITELN ('HELLO')
    END.
```

17. Write a program that will read a sequence of characters typed at the keyboard. The program stops as soon as the letters EUREKA have been typed in this order but not necessarily one after another. For example, the sequence ACEBAK-URAWELMSKA should cause the program to stop.

18. Some computer languages have a slightly more powerful loop statement than FOR. "Translated" into Pascal, this statement would look like this.

    FOR <counter> := <initial value> TO <final value> STEP <increment value>
    DO <statement>

In this construction, the counter is incremented by the increment value rather than by 1, as is in the regular FOR construction, after each iteration. Using a simple example, show how to achieve the same effect with the regular Pascal FOR structure.

19. What is the output of this program segment?

```
    FOR I := 1 TO 10
    DO; WRITELN (I)
```

20. Will the following loop be endless? If not, what will the value of COUNTER be after the loop? PRESENTVALUE and NEXTVALUE are real variables and COUNTER is an integer.

```
    PRESENTVALUE := 1.0;
    NEXTVALUE := 0.5;
    COUNTER := 0;
    REPEAT
        PRESENTVALUE := NEXTVALUE;
        NEXTVALUE := NEXTVALUE / 2;
        COUNTER := COUNTER + 1
    UNTIL PRESENTVALUE = NEXTVALUE
```

Compare the outputs produced by program segments a and b in problems 21 - 24.

21. a. FOR COUNTER := 'C' TO 'F'
     DO WRITELN ('HELLO');
     WRITELN ('GOOD-BYE')

  b. FOR COUNTER := 'C' TO 'F'
     DO BEGIN
        WRITELN ('HELLO');
        WRITELN ('GOOD-BYE')
     END

22. a. FOR COUNTER := 'C' TO 'F'
     DO WRITELN ('HELLO')

  b. FFF := 'F';
     FOR COUNTER := 'C' TO FFF
     DO WRITELN ('HELLO')

23. a. FOR I := 'C' TO 'F'
     DO WRITELN ('HELLO')

  b. FOR I := 'F' DOWNTO 'C'
     DO WRITELN ('HELLO')

24. a. REPEAT
     WRITELN ('HELLO');
     A := SQR (A)
    UNTIL A > B

  b. REPEAT
     BEGIN
        WRITELN ('HELLO');
        A := SQR (A)
     END
    UNTIL A > B

THE GOTO STATEMENT

1. The statement part of a program consists of only two statements:

```
BEGIN
    10:  GOTO 20;
    20:  GOTO 10
END.
```

What will happen during the execution time?

2. Can you think of a simpler program that will have the same effects as the previous one?

3. A program includes the following segment

```
GOTO 1;
A := 0
```

Is there anything peculiar about it?

4. At the dawn of the computer age, programmers often used so-called patches. Here is how that happened. Suppose that after a program had been written the programmer realized that he needed to insert a group of statements in the middle of the program. For reasons that are irrelevant now, the programmer usually inserted in the right place only a statement analogous to the GOTO statement, which

transferred control to the end of the program where all the needed statements were inserted and control was transferred back immediately after the "right" place. Depict the structure of a patched program. What if you have to patch a patch?

Which of the following program segments (5 to 8) are valid and which are not?

5. ```
GOTO 10;
 . . . .
IF A
    THEN 10: <statement 1>
    ELSE <statement 2>
```

6. ```
FOR I := 1 TO 55
DO BEGIN
        . . . . . . . .
      10: <statement>;
        . . . . . . . .
         GOTO 10;
        . . . . . . . .
    END
```

7. ```
REPEAT
      . . . .
      20: <statement>;
      . . . .
UNTIL A;
      . . . .
GOTO 20
```

8. ```
FOR I := -5 DOWNTO -10
DO BEGIN
        . . . . . . . . . .
        GOTO 5;
        . . . . . . . . . .
    END;
 . . . . . . . . . . . .
 5: <statement>
```

9. Take a FOR statement and replace it with an equivalent construction using IF and GOTO statements.

10. Take a WHILE statement and replace it with an equivalent construction using IF and GOTO statements.

11. Take a REPEAT statement and replace it with an equivalent construction using IF and GOTO statements.

12. The GOTO statement has received bad press in computer science literature. While some authors call for dropping it altogether, others advocate its use in a limited number of cases. R. Lawrence Clark in his article "A Linguistic Contribution to GOTO-less Programming," *Commun. ACM*, 27, 4 (April 1984), pp. 349-350, proposed to resolve the debate by introducing a new control statement. The statement has the form

COME FROM <label>

and it causes control to be transferred to the statement immediately following the COME FROM upon completion of the statement labeled <label>. Rewrite the following program segment using COME FROM rather than GOTO statements.

```
            H := 0;
            GOTO 30;
    20:     I := 1;
            J := 2;
            GOTO 40;
    30:     K := 3;
            L := 4;
            GOTO 20;
    40:     M := 5;
            N := 6;
```

Rewrite the following program segments (13 - 15) without using GOTO statements.

13.
```
            SUM := 0;
            FOR I := 1 TO 100
            DO BEGIN
                    SUM := SUM + SQR (3 * I);
                    IF SUM > 200
                        THEN GOTO 10
                END;
    10:     WRITELN (SUM)
```

14.
```
            H := 0;
            GOTO 30;
    20:     I := 1;
            J := 2;
            GOTO 40;
    30:     K := 3;
            L := 4;
            GOTO 20;
    40:     M := 5;
            N := 6;
```

```
15.          IF NUMBER = 1
                 THEN GOTO 10;
             IF NUMBER = 2
                 THEN GOTO 20;
             IF NUMBER = 3
                 THEN GOTO 30;
             IF (NUMBER <> 1) OR (NUMBER <> 2) OR (NUMBER <> 3)
                 THEN GOTO 40;
  10:        A := 100;
             GOTO 50;
  20:        A := 200;
             GOTO 50;
  30:        A := 300;
             GOTO 50;
  40:        A := 400;
  50:        WRITELN (A)
```

4　Program Structure

Functions and procedures are used when it is desirable to break a large and complex program into smaller and more manageable pieces or subroutines, each of which represents a clear-cut part of the whole program. I will use the term *subroutine* to encompass both functions and procedures.

Subroutines are declared right after the variables are declared. There may be several procedures and functions following in an arbitrary order. Moreover, a subroutine may include other subroutines and there are no restrictions on the *depth* of nesting.

Each subroutine begins with a heading. A heading begins with the key word FUNCTION for functions or PROCEDURE for procedures. The next word must be a unique subroutine identifier followed by a parameter list. If it is a function heading, the parameter list is followed by a colon and the type of the function. Here are examples of subroutine headings:

```
PROCEDURE QUADRATICEQUATION(A, B, C : REAL; VAR ROOT1, ROOT2 :
    REAL);
FUNCTION DECIPHER(A : CHAR; KEY : INTEGER) : CHAR;
```

Aside from the heading, a subroutine has the same organization as a program. It may include the declaration of variables, called *local variables*, and the definition of labels, constants, and so on.

Usually, a function is used when a subroutine computes just one value. This value is assigned to the function identifier in the function body. The calling subroutine or program can use a function identifier in any expression. A procedure is used when a subroutine computes several values. The procedure identifier itself is not assigned any value and it is used only to identify the procedure. The first example below shows a function call. The second shows a procedure call.

```
1.  P := 'U';
    CODE := 7;
    Q := DECIPHER (P, CODE);
    WRITELN (P, Q)

2.  COEFFICIENT1 := 1;
    COEFFICIENT2 := -5;
    COEFFICIENT3 := 4;
    QUADRATICEQUATION (COEFFICIENT1, COEFFICIENT2,
                       COEFFICIENT3, X1,X2);
    WRITELN (X1, X2)
```

A subroutine is *invoked* (called) with a list of *actual parameters* that correspond to the *formal parameters* in the subroutine heading. In our example, the procedure call passes the values of COEFFICIENT1, COEFFICIENT2, and COEFFICIENT3 to A, B, and C, respectively. A subroutine may be called several times with different actual parameters, but the number and the types of the actual parameters must agree with the number and the types of the formal parameters.

All identifiers declared in the main program can be referred to in a subroutine, S, unless they are redeclared in S or in a subroutine encompassing S. In this case the identifier declared in the smallest block enclosing S is used in S. No identifier may be used outside the block in which it is declared.

A parameter list consists of two kinds of parameters: *value parameters* and *variable parameters*. When a correspondence between actual and formal parameters is established, there may be two memory allocation schemes. According to the first scheme, a new set of memory locations is created for the formal parameters when a subroutine is invoked. At the time of the subroutine call, the current values of the actual parameters are passed to this new set of memory locations. From then on, the subroutine works only with the new memory locations. According to the second scheme, no new memory locations are created at all. Let us say that A is an actual parameter and X is the corresponding formal parameter. The second scheme simply uses the names A and X as synonyms in the sense that they refer to the same memory location. Any assignment to X in the subroutine will update the value of A.

It is up to the programmer to decide which parameters will employ the first scheme and which will employ the second. These two kinds of parameters are said to be value parameters and variable parameters, respectively. To differentiate between them, the variable parameters are declared in a subroutine heading with the VAR specifier. For example, this formal parameter list

(VAR A, B : REAL; C : CHAR; D : INTEGER; VAR E : CHAR)

declares three variable parameters: A, B and E and two value parameters: C and D.

The main program or a subroutine can call any subroutine declared in it. However, it may not call its "grandchildren" or "great-grandchildren" (and so on). Any subroutine can call its "parent" or "grandparent" (and so on). As for "sibling," the ones declared later may always call the ones declared earlier, but the reverse is not true. Once "sibling" A has the right to call "sibling" B, this right is transferable to all "descendants" of A.

If two subroutines-siblings have to be able to call each other, the subroutine appearing later must be announced before the one appearing earlier. This announcement is accomplished by a dummy declaration which has the form

```
<procedure heading>; FORWARD;
```
or
```
<function heading>; FORWARD;
```

A dummy declaration includes a complete formal parameter list and a function type. When later on the declaration proper appears, it includes the reserved word FUNCTION or PROCEDURE followed by the subroutine identifier only.

In Pascal, a subroutine is allowed to call itself. Such a subroutine is said to be *recursive* or *directly recursive*. Recursive subroutines may be elegant solutions to some problems.

FUNCTIONS

1. What is performed by the following function?

```
FUNCTION EVEN (NUMBER: INTEGER): BOOLEAN;
BEGIN
    EVEN := NOT ODD (NUMBER)
END;
```

2. Write a program that prompts the user to enter a letter, then calls a function that determines whether the letter is a vowel or a consonant and prints an appropriate message. Verify that the entered character is a letter.

3. Write a program that prompts the user to enter the coordinates of two points, then calls a function to compute the distance between the points and prints the distance.

4. MYSTERY (A, B) is a user declared function. Which of the following assignment statements may appear within the body of the main program?

```
a. X := MYSTERY (1, 2)
b. X := MYSTERY (1, M)
c. X := MYSTERY (X, Y)
```

d. X := MYSTERY (X, X)
e. X := MYSTERY (SQR (L), M)
f. X := MYSTERY (ABS (4 - C))
g. X := MYSTERY (3, A) - MYSTERY (4, 0)
h. X := SQR (MYSTERY (ABS (A), ABS (B)))
i. X := MYSTERY (MYSTERY (A, B), -C)
j. X := MYSTERY (MYSTERY (1, 2) + MYSTERY (2, 1),
                            3 - MYSTERY (0, 0))

5. MYSTERY (A, B) is a user declared function. May the following statement appear in the body of the main program?

    MYSTERY (1, 2) := 0

6. May a function have two formal parameters of different types?

7. FUN (X) is a function. What is the difference between the output of this program segment

    A := 'C';
    WRITE (FUN (A))

and this one

    WRITE (FUN ('C'))

Find the error in each of the next three examples.

8.   FUNCTION SECONDNEXT(C : CHAR) : CHAR;
      VAR
          NEXT : CHAR;
      BEGIN
          NEXT := CHR (ORD (C) + 1);
          NEXT := CHR (ORD (NEXT) + 1)
      END;

9.   PROGRAM ONE (...
      . . . .
      FUNCTION FUNCONE (A, B : INTEGER) : REAL;
      BEGIN {of FUNCONE}
          . . . .
      END; {of FUNCONE}
      BEGIN {of main program}
      . . . .
          Z := FUNCONE (X) DIV 12;
      . . . .

```
        END. {of main program}
10.     PROGRAM TWO (...
        ................
        FUNCTION FUNCTWO (A, B : INTEGER) : REAL;
        BEGIN {of FUNCTWO}
        ................
        END; {of FUNCTWO}
        BEGIN {of main program}
            ................
            Z := FUNCTWO (X, 3.14) / 1.2;
            ................
        END. {of main program}
```

11. May the body of a function be empty?

12. The following declaration appears in a program.

```
    FUNCTION MYSTERY (A, B, C : INTEGER) : INTEGER;
    BEGIN
        MYSTERY := 3 * A - 4 * B DIV C
    END;
```

What will the value of K be after execution of the following statements?

```
a. K := MYSTERY (1, 2, 3)
b. K := MYSTERY (1, 2, 1) - MYSTERY (0, 1, 1)
c. K := MYSTERY (1, MYSTERY (1, 2, 3), -1)
```

13. The declaration below appears in a program

```
    FUNCTION EXP (X : REAL) : REAL;
    BEGIN
        EXP := LN (X)
    END;
```

Is this declaration valid and, if so, what will be assigned to A after execution of this statement

```
    A := EXP (1.0)
```

in the main program?

14. A programmer replaced this declaration

```
FUNCTION A (B : REAL) : INTEGER;
BEGIN
    A := TRUNC (B) + 1
END;
```

with this one

```
FUNCTION A (BBB : REAL) : INTEGER;
BEGIN
    A := TRUNC (BBB) + 1
END;
```

while the main program was left intact. Can that make any difference at run time?

15. May a function have no parameters at all?

16. It is perfectly legal to use the same identifier in an actual parameter list more than once. Is it legal to use the same identifier in a formal parameter list more than once? For example, this statement is valid:

```
A := B (X, X)
```

How about this function heading:

```
FUNCTION D (M, M : INTEGER) : CHAR;
```

Explain the answer.

17. The formal parameter list of function MYSTERY consists of the identifiers A, B and C, in that order. Can the following statement appear in the main program?

```
X := MYSTERY (B, C, A)
```

18. A function has two parameters. A programmer decided to reverse their order in the function heading. What else has to be changed to keep the behavior of the program intact?

19. May an actual parameter list and the corresponding formal parameter list consist of the same names in the same order?

20. May a formal parameter list includes variable of these types:

a. CHAR
b. ARRAY
c. RECORD

21. The body of a function includes the following statement:

A := 0

where A is a local variable.
The function is invoked twice. May we assume that by the time of the second call A has already been initialized?

22. The formal parameter A is declared as real. May the actual parameter corresponding to A be X [4], where A is an array of real numbers?

23. May a user declared function be of the following types?

   a. CHAR
   b. ARRAY
   c. REAL
   d. RECORD
   e. user-defined ordinal type
   f. pointer

PROCEDURES

1. Would you write a function or a procedure to convert the rectangular coordinates of a point to its polar coordinates?

2. PROC is a procedure. May the following statement appear in the main program?

```
A := 2 * PROC (0, 7)
```

3. Is it always possible to divide the procedure parameters into two nonintersecting groups, input and output parameters?

4. Explain what the following program does.

```
PROGRAM MYSTERY1 (INPUT, OUTPUT);
TYPE
      STRING = PACKED ARRAY [1..20] OF CHAR;
VAR
      BEFORE, AFTER : STRING;

      I : INTEGER;
PROCEDURE PUZZLE1 (FIRST : STRING; VAR SECOND : STRING);
      CONST
         KEY = 3;
      VAR
         J : INTEGER;
      BEGIN { of procedure}
```

```
          FOR J := 1 TO 20
          DO SECOND [J] := CHR ((ORD (FIRST [J]) - ORD ('A')
                                    + KEY) MOD 26 + ORD ('A'))
     END; {of procedure}
BEGIN {of main program}
     WRITELN ('ENTER A STRING OF 20 LETTERS');
     FOR I := 1 TO 20
     DO READ (BEFORE [I]);
     PUZZLE1 (BEFORE, AFTER);
     WRITELN (AFTER)
END. {of main program}
```

5. Modify the preceding program in the following way. All 26 letters are arbitrarily broken into 13 pairs: (A1, B1), (A2, B2), . . ., (A13, B13) and each A is replaced by the corresponding B and vice versa.

Find the error in each of the next two procedures.

6.
```
PROCEDURE PUZZLE2 (A : CHAR; VAR B : CHAR);
BEGIN
    B := CHR (ORD (A) + 1);
    PUZZLE2 := B
END;
```

7.
```
PROCEDURE PUZZLE3 (X : 1..100; VAR Y : INTEGER);
BEGIN
    Y := 2 * X
END;
```

8. Can there be a procedure without parameters?

Find the error in each of the next four program segments.

9.
```
PROCEDURE SECRET1 (A : INTEGER);
BEGIN

    .
    .
    .

END; { OF SECRET1 }
BEGIN { OF MAIN PROGRAM }
    .
    .
    .
    SECRET1 ('A');
    .
```

```
                .
        END. { OF MAIN PROGRAM }

10.     PROCEDURE SECRET2 (A, B : INTEGER);
        BEGIN
             .
             .
             .
        END; { OF SECRET2 }
        BEGIN { OF MAIN PROGRAM }
             .
             .
             .
           SECRET2 (2, 4, 0);
             .
             .
             .
        END. { OF MAIN PROGRAM }

11.     PROCEDURE SECRET3 (VAR A, B : REAL);
        BEGIN
             .
             .
             .
        END; { OF SECRET3 }
        BEGIN { OF MAIN PROGRAM }
             .
             .
             .
           SECRET3 (3, M);
             .
             .
             .
        END. { OF MAIN PROGRAM }

12.     PROCEDURE SECRET4 (A : REAL; VAR B : REAL);
        BEGIN
             .
             .
             .
        END; { OF SECRET4 }
        BEGIN { OF MAIN PROGRAM }
             .
             .
```

```
                    .
        X := 1.0;
        Y := 2.0;
        SECRET4 (X + Y, X - Y);
                    .
                    .
                    .
    END. { OF MAIN PROGRAM }
```

13. What will be printed by this program?

```
    PROGRAM SECRET5 (OUTPUT);
    VAR
        A, B, C : INTEGER;
    PROCEDURE MYSTERY5;
        VAR
            B : INTEGER;
        BEGIN { OF MYSTERY5 }
            A := 1;
            B := 2;
            C := 3
        END; { OF MYSTERY5 }
    BEGIN { OF MAIN PROGRAM }
        A := 101;
        B := 102;
        C := 103;
        MYSTERY5;
        WRITELN (A, B, C)
    END. { OF MAIN PROGRAM }
```

Depict the output of the next four programs.

14.
```
    PROGRAM ONE (OUTPUT);
    VAR
        A, B : INTEGER;
    PROCEDURE PROCONE (C, D);
        BEGIN { OF PROCONE }
            C := A + B;
            D := A - B;
            WRITELN (C, D)
        END; { OF PROCONE }
    BEGIN { OF MAIN PROGRAM }
        A := 1;
        B := 2;
```

```
        PROCONE (A, B)
    END. { OF MAIN PROGRAM }

15.     PROGRAM TWO (OUTPUT);
    VAR
        A, B : INTEGER;
    PROCEDURE PROCTWO (X, Y : INTEGER);
        BEGIN { OF PROCTWO }
            X := A + B;
            Y := A - B
        END; { OF PROCTWO }
    BEGIN { OF MAIN PROGRAM }
        A := 1;
        B := 2;
        PROCTWO (A, B);
        WRITELN (A, B)
    END. { OF MAIN PROGRAM }

16.     PROGRAM THREE (OUTPUT);
    VAR
        A, B : INTEGER;
    PROCEDURE PROCTHREE (X : INTEGER; VAR Y : INTEGER);
        BEGIN { OF PROCTHREE }
            X := A + B;
            Y := A - B
        END; { OF PROCTHREE }
    BEGIN { OF MAIN PROGRAM }
        A := 1;
        B := 2;
        PROCTHREE (A, B);
        WRITELN (A, B)
    END. { OF MAIN PROGRAM }

17.     PROGRAM FOUR (OUTPUT);
    VAR
        A, B : INTEGER;
    PROCEDURE PROCFOUR (VAR X, Y : INTEGER);
        BEGIN { OF PROCFOUR }
            X := 3;
            Y := 4
        END; { OF PROCFOUR }
    BEGIN { OF MAIN PROGRAM }
        A := 1;
        B := 2;
        PROCFOUR (A, B);
```

```
            WRITELN (A, B)
      END. { OF MAIN PROGRAM }
```

18. Which of the parameters listed in the following procedure heading are value parameters and which are variable parameters?

```
PROCEDURE X (VAR A, B : CHAR; C, D : BOOLEAN;
                           VAR E : REAL);
```

19. What is the difference between these two procedure calls

```
PROC (A, B)
```

and

```
PROC ('A', B)
```

if the heading for procedure PROC is

```
PROC (X : CHAR; VAR Y : BOOLEAN);
```

20. Give an example demonstrating that a program may compute different results if value parameters of a procedure are changed to variable parameters.

BLOCK STRUCTURE AND SCOPE

1. Give an example of the skeleton of a program with two procedures declared on the same level.

2. Can a function be declared within a procedure?

3. Can a procedure be declared within a function?

4. Depict the skeleton of a program with two functions one of which is declared within the other.

Program A includes procedures B, C, D and E arranged as shown in Fig. 4-1.

The following variables are declared in the variable declaration parts:

in program A:	K, L, M, N
in procedure B:	K, L, O, P, R
in procedure C:	K, P, S
in procedure D:	M, R, S, T
in procedure E:	N, R

Let us assume, for the sake of simplicity, that all procedures have no parameters. Given

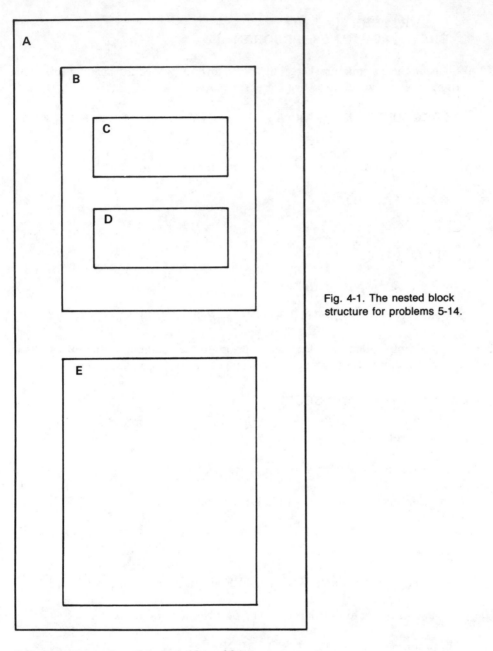

Fig. 4-1. The nested block structure for problems 5-14.

this structure, solve the next 10 problems.

5. K is assigned a value in A and procedure B is invoked. May we assume that the value of K is known in B?

6. L is assigned a value in B and procedure D is invoked. Is the value of L available in D?

7. The following sequence of steps has been executed:

- L is assigned a value in A.
- A invokes B.
- L is assigned a new value in B.
- B invokes C.

Which value of L is available in C?

8. The following sequence of steps has been executed:

- A invokes B.
- B invokes C.
- S is assigned a value in C.
- Control is transferred back to B.
- B invokes D.

Is the value of S known in D?

9. The following sequence of steps has been executed:

- R is assigned a value in E.
- Control is transferred back to A.
- A invokes B.
- B invokes D.

Is the value of R known in D?

10. R is assigned a value in E and control is transferred back to A. Is the value of R available in A?

11. May A call C directly?

12. May D call C?

13. May C call B?

14. May B call E?

Each of the next seven problems includes a GOTO statement. To which statement will control be transferred after execution of the GOTO statement?

15.   `PROGRAM FIRST ( ...`
       `LABEL 10;`
          .
          .

```
        .
FUNCTION FIRSTFUNCTION (...
   LABEL 10;
   BEGIN { OF FIRSTFUNCTION }
        .
        .
        .
      GOTO 10;
        .
        .
        .
      10: <statement 1>;
   END; { OF FIRSTFUNCTION }
BEGIN { OF MAIN PROGRAM }
     .
     .
     .
   10: <statement 2>;
     .
     .
     .
END. { OF MAIN PROGRAM }
```

16.
```
PROGRAM SECOND (...
LABEL 10;
     .
     .
     .
FUNCTION SECONDFUNCTION (...
   LABEL 10;
   BEGIN { OF SECONDFUNCTION }
        .
        .
        .
      GOTO 10;
        .
        .
        .
   END; { OF SECONDFUNCTION }
BEGIN { OF MAIN PROGRAM }
     .
     .
     .
   10: <statement 2>;
     .
```

```
                    .
                    .
           END. { OF MAIN PROGRAM }

17.        PROGRAM THIRD (...
           LABEL 10;
                 .
                 .
                 .
           FUNCTION THIRDFUNCTION (...
              LABEL 10;
              BEGIN { OF THIRDFUNCTION }
                    .
                    .
                    .
                 10: <statement 1>;
              END; { OF THIRDFUNCTION }
           BEGIN { OF MAIN PROGRAM }
                 .
                 .
                 .
              GOTO 10;
                 .
                 .
                 .
              10: <statement 2>;
                 .
                 .
                 .
           END. { OF MAIN PROGRAM }

18.        PROGRAM FOURTH (...
           LABEL 10;
                 .
                 .
                 .
           FUNCTION FOURTHFUNCTION (...
              LABEL 10;
              BEGIN { OF FOURTHFUNCTION }
                    .
                    .
                    .
                 10: <statement 1>;
              END; { OF FOURTHFUNCTION }
           BEGIN { OF MAIN PROGRAM }
                 .
```

```
            .
            .
        GOTO 10;
            .

            .
            .
        END. { OF MAIN PROGRAM }

19.     PROGRAM FIFTH (...
        LABEL 10;
            .
            .
            .
        FUNCTION FIFTHFUNCTION (...
            BEGIN { OF FIFTHFUNCTION }
                .
                .
                .
            GOTO 10;
                .
                .
                .
            10: <statement 1>;
            END; { OF FIFTHFUNCTION }
        BEGIN { OF MAIN PROGRAM }
            .
            .
            .
        10: <statement 2>;
            .
            .
            .
20.     PROGRAM SIXTH (...
        LABEL 10;
            .
            .
            .
        FUNCTION SIXTHFUNCTION (...
            BEGIN { OF SIXTHFUNCTION }
                .
                .
                .
            GOTO 10;
                .
                .
                .
```

```
            END; { OF SIXTHFUNCTION }
            BEGIN { OF MAIN PROGRAM }
                    .
                    .
                    .
            10: <statement 2>;
                    .
                    .
                    .
            END. { OF MAIN PROGRAM }

21.     PROGRAM SEVENTH (...
        LABEL 10;
                .
                .
                .
        FUNCTION SEVENTHFUNCTION (...
            BEGIN { OF SEVENTHFUNCTION }
                    .
                    .
                    .
                10: <statement 1>;
            END; { OF SEVENTHFUNCTION }
        BEGIN { OF MAIN PROGRAM }
                .
                .
                .
            GOTO 10;
                .
                .
                .
        END. { OF MAIN PROGRAM }
```

22. A program has the following skeleton:

```
        PROGRAM X ...
            .
            .
            .
        PROCEDURE Y ...
                .
                .
                .
            BEGIN { OF Y }
```

```
        •
        •
        •
     END;  { OF Y }
  PROCEDURE  Z ...
        •
        •
        •
     BEGIN  { OF Z }
        •
        •
        •
     END;  { OF Z }
  BEGIN  { OF X }
        •
        •
        •
  END.  { OF X }
```

Add a FORWARD declaration that will allow each procedure to invoke the other.

A program has the structure shown in Fig. 4-2. A FORWARD declaration is used, so that B may call D and vice versa. Under these conditions answer the next eight questions.

23. May B call E?

24. May D call C?

25. May E call B?

26. May C call D?

27. May C call E?

28. May E call C?

29. May B call D if D, in turn, calls B?

30. May B call B itself?

31. Write a program that reads the elements of an array of 5 integer numbers and then calls a function that computes the product of the elements recursively. Describe each step of the computations.

32. Solve the previous problem using a nonrecursive function.

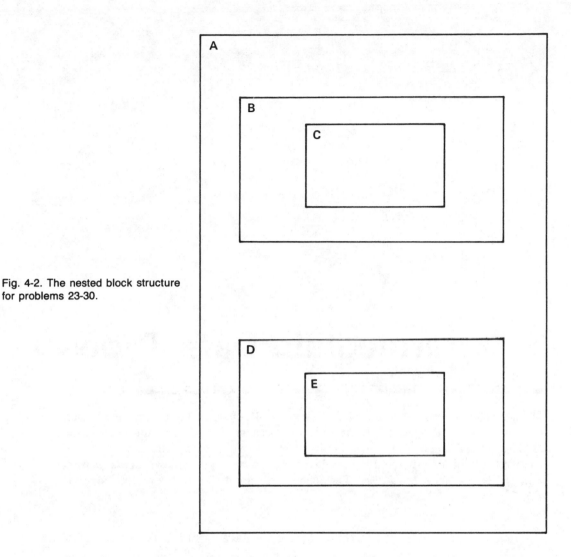

Fig. 4-2. The nested block structure for problems 23-30.

33. Write a program that reads the elements of an array of 5 real numbers and then calls a procedure that finds the maximum of the elements and the position of the maximum element recursively.

34. Solve the previous problem using a nonrecursive procedure.

5 Intermediate Data Types

The nature of some variables is such that they can take on only a finite number of values, such as days of the week, counties in a state, or car models. Such values can be encoded by integer numbers, but it would be more natural to use the original values themselves. This brings about the need to introduce new types known as *user-defined ordinal types* or *enumerated types*. The following example illustrates the introduction of a new type:

```
TYPE
    TRANSPORTATION = (CAR, CART, TRAIN, BUS, TRUCK);
VAR
    VEHICLE : TRANSPORTATION;
```

The variable VEHICLE can take five values enumerated in its type definition.

Having declared the variable VEHICLE, we can write such statements as

```
VEHICLE := BUS
```

or

```
IF VEHICLE = CAR
    THEN SPEED := 55
```

User-declared ordinal variables can be used in any control statement. However, they cannot be arguments in READ, READLN, WRITE, or WRITELN procedures.

The function ORD is defined for any ordinal argument and it returns its ordinal number. Note that the ordinal number of the first value is 0 rather than 1. Two other standard functions provided by Pascal for all ordinal types are PRED and SUCC, which return the predecessor and successor of the arguments, respectively.

In many applications, all possible values of a variable make up only a subrange of the full range of a previously defined type. If so, its type can be defined as a *subrange*, whereas the previously defined type is referred to as the *host type*. Here are several examples of subrange declarations:

```
TYPE
   DAY = (SUNDAY, MONDAY, TUESDAY, WEDNESDAY,
          THURSDAY, FRIDAY, SATURDAY);
VAR
   WEEKDAY : MONDAY..FRIDAY;
   WARYEARS : 1939..1945;
   LUCKYLETTERS : 'I'..'N';
```

The variable WARYEARS, for instance, can take all integer values between 1939 and 1945, inclusive.

The type ARRAY is a structured type consisting of a fixed number of homogeneous components. The definition of arrays looks like this:

```
TYPE
   X = ARRAY[10..20] OF REAL;
   Y = ARRAY['I'..'N'] OF INTEGER;
   Z = ARRAY[1..10,1..20] OF CHAR;
VAR
   A : X;
   B : Y;
   C : Z;
```

According to these declarations,

- A is an array consisting of 11 real components or elements;
- B is an array consisting of 6 integer components;
- C is a two dimensional array consisting of 10 by 20 or 200 components.

Individual components of an array are referred to as A[12], B['K'], C[1,15], A[3 * 5] or B [PRED('E')].

It is possible sometimes to reduce the amount of memory required to store an array by squeezing two or more components into one memory location. Such arrays are called *packed*. Here is the definition of a packed array type:

```
TYPE
   NAME = PACKED ARRAY[1..20] OF CHAR;
```

A *string* is a one dimensional packed array of characters with a lower bound of 1. Pascal has two facilities applicable to strings but not applicable to arrays in general: a string identifier with no subscripts can be an argument of WRITE and WRITELN (but not READ or READLN) procedures, and a value can be assigned to a string directly. To wit:

```
NAME := 'JOHN SMITH'
```

is a valid assignment if NAME is a string with ten components.

A *set* is a structured variable that is a collection of scalar values of the same type, which is referred to as the *base* type. Sets can be declared like this:

```
TYPE
   DAY = (SUNDAY, MONDAY, TUESDAY, WEDNESDAY, THURSDAY,
          FRIDAY, SATURDAY);
   WARYEARS : 1939..1945;
   DAYSOFDEPARTURE = SET OF DAY;
   YEARSOFBIRTH = SET OF WARYEARS;
   CHARACTERS = SET OF CHAR;
VAR
   SHIPDEPARTURES, TRAINDEPARTURES : DAYSOFDEPARTURE;
   YEARSREPRESENTED : YEARSOFBIRTH;
   GOODCHARACTERS, BADCHARACTERS : CHARACTERS;
```

Having declared these set characters, we can make the following assignments:

```
GOODCHARACTERS := ['A', 'E', 'I,' 'O', 'U', 'Y'];
BADCHARACTERS := ['B', 'C', 'D'];
YEARSREPRESENTED := [1942, 1943];
SHIPDEPARTURES := [MONDAY, THURSDAY];
```

Specific implementations impose restrictions on the number of elements in a set. The order of the elements in a set is unimportant and two sets are said to be equal if they contain the same elements.

Three operations defined for sets; *union, intersection,* and *difference*, are analogous to their counterparts in mathematics. They are denoted as A + B, A * B, and A – B, respectively, and they have the same precedence as their arithmetic counterparts. A set can be assigned an empty value:

```
A := [ ]
```

Five relational operators can be used to compare sets:

operator	meaning	example
=	equal	[2, 5, 6] = [5, 6] (which yields FALSE)
< >	not equal	A < > [ ] (which yields TRUE if A is not empty)
> =	contains	[MONDAY, TUESDAY, FRIDAY] > =

		[TUESDAY, FRIDAY] (which yields TRUE)
< =	is contained	A < = B (TRUE if all elements of A are also elements of B)
IN	test member-ship of an element in a set	B IN [1940 . . . 1950] (which is TRUE if the current value of B is within that range)

Finally, a file is a structured type which is a collection of values of the same type accessible only sequentially. Unlike an array, a file does not have a fixed number of components. While variables of all other types (real, integer, arrays, sets) are created at run-time and they cease to exist after the program has run, a file can exist independently of the program that accesses it.

Files can be declared as follows:

```
TYPE
   GRADES = FILE OF INTEGER;
VAR
   SECTION1GRADES, SECTION2GRADES : GRADES;
```

TEXT is a file of characters, and it is a predefined type in Pascal. Files that exist independently of the program that accesses them are called *external files* and their identifiers must be named in the program heading. Files that are created by a program and deleted after the program has run are called *internal* or *scratch files*. Internal files are not named in the program heading.

Once a file has been declared, a variable capable of holding one element of the file and called the file buffer is automatically created. This variable is denoted by the file name followed by an up-arrow or caret.

The following standard functions are defined for all files (F is a file name):

• REWRITE (F) prepares file F for writing. If F already exists, its contents are erased.
• PUT (F) appends the value of the buffer to the end of file F. It is assumed that some value has been assigned to the buffer.
• WRITE (F, X) combines two operations: it assigns the value of X to the buffer and puts or appends the value of the buffer to the end of F.
• RESET (F) prepares file F for reading. The value of the first component of the file is assigned to the buffer.
• GET (F) assigns the value of the next component of file F to the buffer.
• READ (F, X) assigns the value of the next component of file F to variable X.

If the GET or READ procedure is applied after the file buffer has already been equal to the last component of file F, the standard function EOF (F) is set TRUE and the buffer is left undefined. At all other times EOF (F) is FALSE.

As we have said, a text file is a file of characters. However, if the statement

READ (F, X)

is encountered, where F is a text file and X is an integer or real variable, a whole group of characters is read and converted to the integer or real form, respectively. If the statement

```
WRITE (F, X)
```

is encountered, where F is a text file and X is a real or integer variable, the representation of X is converted to a group of characters that are appended to file F.

All characters of a text file are organized into lines. If the GET or READ procedure is applied after the file buffer has already been equal to the last character of a line, the standard function EOLN (F) is set TRUE and the buffer is left undefined. At all other times EOLN (F) is FALSE.

The standard functions READLN and WRITELN are defined for text files only. They are analogous to the standard functions READLN and WRITELN that are used with the files INPUT and OUTPUT and described in Chapter 1. However, if they are used with an arbitrary file, the name of the file must be the first argument of the procedure.

USER-DEFINED ORDINAL TYPES

1. Declare a variable whose values are RED, ORANGE, YELLOW, GREEN, BLUE, INDIGO, VIOLET.

2. Can a constant of a user-defined type appear in the constant definition part of the main program?

3. Assuming these definitions and declarations:

```
TYPE
    SPECTRUM = (RED, ORANGE, YELLOW, GREEN, BLUE, INDIGO,
               VIOLET);
VAR
    COLOR : SPECTRUM;
```

evaluate

a. ORD (RED)
b. ORD (VIOLET)
c. PRED (YELLOW)
d. SUCC (GREEN)
e. PRED (PRED (BLUE))
f. SUCC (PRED (ORANGE))
g. SUCC (VIOLET)
h. ORD (SUCC (PRED (RED)))

4. Redeclare the variable COLOR in the previous problem without defining its type.

5. Is the type VOWELS defined below valid?

```
TYPE
    VOWELS = ('A', 'E', 'I', 'O', 'U', 'Y');
```

Explain the answer.

6. The variable MONTH has been declared as follows:

```
TYPE
    MONTHTYPE = (JAN, FEB, MAR, APR, MAY, JUN,
                 JUL, AUG, SEP, OCT, NOV, DEC);
VAR
    MONTH : MONTHTYPE;
```

and it has been assigned a value. Write a program segment that will print the value.

7. Give an example of a FOR loop wherein the control variable has a user-defined type.

8. The standard function ORD returns the position of a value of any enumerated type. However, the inverse function, CHR, is defined for character variables only. Write a program segment that will convert the ordinal position of a value to the value itself.

9. The variable LETTER is declared as follows:

```
TYPE
    LETTER = 'A'..'Z';
VAR
    LETTER1, LETTER2 : LETTER;
```

Is the statement

```
WRITELN (LETTER1, LETTER2)
```

valid?

10. Which of these type definitions are valid and which are not?

```
a. TYPE A = 10..MAX;
b. TYPE B = 10..10;
c. TYPE C = 10..5;
d. TYPE D = 0..SQR (10);
e. TYPE E = 1.0..10.0;
f. TYPE F = '1'..'5';
g. TYPE G = 1..'5';
```

11. Can a type be defined as a subrange of:

a. REAL
b. INTEGER
c. CHAR
d. any user-defined ordinal type
e. ARRAY
f. SET
g. FILE
h. RECORD

12. N is an integer variable and M is a subrange:

```
TYPE
    MTYPE = -20..-10;
VAR
    M : MTYPE;
```

Which of the following assignment statements is/are valid?

```
a. N  := M
b. M  := N
c. N  := ABS (M)
d. N  := N + M
```

ARRAYS AND STRINGS

1. List all elements of each of the following arrays:

```
a. TYPE
      ATYPE = ARRAY [1..10] OF INTEGER;
   VAR
      A : ATYPE;
b. TYPE
      BTYPE = ARRAY [-5..0] OF CHAR;
   VAR
      B : BTYPE;
c. TYPE
      CTYPE = ARRAY ['N'..'R'] OF REAL;
   VAR
      C : CTYPE;
d. TYPE
      STATES = (CA, OR, WA, NV, NM, AZ);
      POPULACE = ARRAY [CA..WA] OF INTEGER;
   VAR
      POPULATION : POPULACE;
e. TYPE
      ETYPE = ARRAY [3..5, -2..0] OF CHAR;
```

```
      VAR
          E : ETYPE;
   f. TYPE
          CHAIRS = ARRAY [1..3, 'A'..'C'] OF BOOLEAN;
      VAR
          SEATS : CHAIRS;
   g. TYPE
          CUBE = ARRAY [0..1, 0..1, 0..1] OF BOOLEAN;
      VAR
          VERTICES : CUBE;
   h. TYPE
          TYPEOFRESPONSE = ARRAY [BOOLEAN, BOOLEAN]
                              OF BOOLEAN;
      VAR
          RESPONSE : TYPEOFRESPONSE;
   i. TYPE
          A = (X, Y, Z);
          ITYPE = ARRAY [BOOLEAN, A] OF CHAR;
      VAR
          I : ITYPE;
```

2. Redeclare the arrays used in the previous problem without separately defining their types.

3. Comment on these type declarations:

```
   a. TYPE
          ATYPE = ARRAY [1..MAX] OF INTEGER;
   b. TYPE
          BTYPE = ARRAY [10..10] OF REAL;
   c. TYPE
          CTYPE = ARRAY [10..5] OF BOOLEAN;
   d. TYPE
          DTYPE = ARRAY [0..SQR(10)] OF CHAR;
   e. TYPE
          ETYPE = ARRAY [1.0..10.0] OF INTEGER;
   f. TYPE
          FTYPE = ARRAY ['1'..'5'] OF REAL;
   g. TYPE
          GTYPE = ARRAY [1..'5'] OF BOOLEAN;
   h. TYPE
          HTYPE = ARRAY [CHAR] OF CHAR;
   i. TYPE
          ITYPE = ARRAY [INTEGER] OF REAL;
```

j. TYPE
        JTYPE = ARRAY [BOOLEAN] OF INTEGER;

4. The array NUMBERS contains 100 real numbers. Write a program segment that will compute the differences between every two consecutive numbers and put them in the array DIFFERENCES.

5. Comment on the validity of these expressions:

   a. A [X + Y]
   b. B [SQR (Z)]
   c. C [M [N]]
   d. D [ROUND (3.14)]

6. Two users play tic-tac-toe by typing their moves, such as 2 1, at a terminal. A program checks the validity of each move and announces the winner. Write such a program.

7. Write a program that will ask for 10 real numbers, store them in an array and compute their mean and standard deviation.

8. Write a program segment that will locate and print the minimum and the maximum of a two dimensional array, as well as the positions of the minimum and maximum elements. If there are several minimum or maximum elements, consider the following versions:

   • The program prints the position of the first element among them (the one in the minimum row and in the minimum column within the same row).
   • The program prints the position of the last element among them.
   • The program prints the positions of all such elements.

9. X is an array of real numbers. Write a program that will compute their histogram.

10. Y is an array of real numbers. Write a program that will compute and print the largest 10 percent of its elements.

11. Can an entire array (without its subscripts) be passed as a parameter to a function or a procedure?

12. A and B are arrays of real numbers and they have the same number of elements. Is the statement

    A := B

    valid?

13. MATRIX is a two dimensional array declared as follows:

```
TYPE
    TYPEOFMATRIX = ARRAY[1..N, 1..N] OF INTEGER;
VAR
    MATRIX : TYPEOFMATRIX;
```

Write a program segment that will check whether MATRIX is symmetrical or not. (A two dimensional array, A, is symmetrical if A [I, J] = A [J, I] for all pairs I and J.)

14. Write a program that will compute all prime numbers below 1000.

15. Which of these statements are correct and which are not?

   a. A packed array occupies four times less memory than its unpacked counterpart.
   b. A program using packed arrays executes more slowly than the same program using unpacked arrays.
   c. Only arrays of characters can be packed arrays.
   d. Individual elements of packed arrays are not accessible.

16. Can a string variable be an argument of the procedures READ, READLN, WRITE and WRITELN?

17. S is a string variable consisting of 10 characters. Which, if any, statements below are valid?

```
a. S := 'ABC'
b. S := 'AAABBBCCCD'
c. S := 'AAAABBBBCCCCDDDD'
```

18. Write a program that will read a ten letter word and then print it backward.

SETS

1. Declare a set variable called HOBBIES that contains these values:

   - HIKING
   - MOVIE GOING
   - READING
   - TABLE TENNIS
   - MUSIC
   - POLITICS

2. How many different values can the variable ROOMS declared below have?

```
TYPE
    LISTOFROOMS = (LIVINGROOM, DININGROOM,
                   BEDROOM, KITCHEN);
```

```
     TYPEOFROOMS = SET OF LISTOFROOMS;
   VAR
       ROOMS : TYPEOFROOMS;
```

3. What is the error in the following definition:

```
   TYPE
       FRACTIONS = SET OF REAL;
```

4. What is the error in this definition:

```
   TYPE
       NUMBERS = SET OF INTEGER;
```

5. Evaluate X if

```
   A is ['A', 'C', 'F', 'U']
   B is ['C', 'D', 'E', 'F', 'G', 'H']
   C is ['F', 'M', 'P']
```

```
   a. X := A + B
   b. X := B * C
   c. X := A - C
   d. X := C + A * B
   e. X := (C + A) * B
   f. X := A - A
   g. X := A + A * A - A
```

6. Evaluate the following Boolean expressions:

```
   a. A = B
   b. B <> C
   c. D >= B
   d. C <= E
   e. 'A' IN ['I'..'N']
```

where

```
   A is ['K', 'L', 'M', 'N']
   B is ['L', 'N', 'M', 'K']
   C is ['I'..'P']
   D is []
   E is ['K']
```

7. Evaluate this Boolean expression:

```
   [1..10] = [1..5, 6..10]
```

8. Evaluate this Boolean expression:

```
[1, 2, 3] < [1, 2, 3, 4]
```

9. A set has been declared as follows:

```
TYPE
    LISTOFSTATES = (CA, OR, WA, NV, NM, AZ);
    TYPEOFSTATES = SET OF LISTOFSTATES;
VAR
    STATES : TYPEOFSTATES;
```

and a value has been assigned to STATES. Write a program segment that will compute the number of members of the set assigned to STATES.

10. What is wrong with the following statement if HOBBIES is a set variable and MUSIC is an element of that set?

```
HOBBIES := HOBBIES + MUSIC
```

11. Can a set constant appear in the constant definition part of the main program?

12. Is the following statement valid?

```
A := [PRED ('Y'), 'Y', SUCC ('Y')]
```

13. Two people are said to be compatible if they have some interests in common. Write a program that will determine whether two people are compatible. Each person should enter a set of his or her hobbies and if the intersection of the two sets contains at least three members, then they are compatible. (Needless to say that the same problem arises in employment agencies, which try to match up job seekers with openings reasonably well, and in real estate agencies, which match up buyers with sellers.)

14. Sets A and B consist of M and N members, respectively. What is the range for the number of members in

a. A + B
b. A * B
c. A - B

15. Simplify this statement:

```
IF (A = 3) OR (A = 4) OR (A = 5) OR (A = 6)
   OR (A = 8)
    THEN <statement 1>
    ELSE <statement 2>
```

16. Some of the vegetables from this list:

    artichoke
    asparagus
    beans
    broccoli
    eggplant
    tomato

    are grown in some of the Western states:

    California
    Oregon
    Washington
    Nevada
    New Mexico
    Arizona.

    Declare an array of sets appropriate for this situation and assign some values to this array.

17. Assuming the declaration made in the previous problem, write a program segment that will print out the values of the array.

FILES

1. Can the components of a file be
   a. arrays
   b. records
   c. files
   d. arrays of records

2. Two programs are identical except for their headings, which are

    ```
    PROGRAM FIRST (INPUT, OUTPUT, A, B, C);
    ```
    and
    ```
    PROGRAM SECOND (A, C, INPUT, B, OUTPUT);
    ```

    How important is this difference?

3. A program produces real numbers and stores them in a file. Does the file have to be a FILE OF REAL?

4. May a line of a text file consist of 0 characters?

5. F is a FILE OF INTEGER. Can we use the WRITELN statement to write to F?

6. What file does not require a REWRITE call before writing to it?

7. Find the error in this program segment:

```
RESET (F);
READ (F, X);
IF X < 0
    THEN WRITE (F, X)
    ELSE WRITE (F, -X)
```

8. Can data be written to the file INPUT?

9. The statement

```
WRITELN (X)
```

seems ambiguous. It can be interpreted either as "write the value of the variable X to OUTPUT," or as "go to the next line in file X." How is this ambiguity resolved?

10. Can a file be passed as a parameter to a procedure or a function?

11. Files A and B have the same type. Is the statement

```
A := B
```

valid?

12. Write a program that will create a text file consisting of the first 100 lines of a given text file. If the given file has fewer than 100 lines, all its lines should be copied to the new file.

13. Write a program that will create a text file consisting of all odd-numbered lines of a given text file.

14. Write a program that will determine whether or not two files of integers are identical.

15. Write a program that will append a file of reals to the end of another file of reals.

16. A word is a group of letters (characters A through Z) enclosed between two blank characters, between a blank and the end of a line, or between the beginning of a line and a blank. Write a program that will delete all four letter words from a text file.

17. Write a program that will count the number of lines and the number of characters in a text file.

18. Write a program that will transform a text file as follows: if there is more than one blank character after a period, a question mark, or an exclamation point, all

blank characters but one are deleted. For example,

Hi!   How are you?   I am fine.

becomes

Hi! How are you? I am fine.

19. A text file consists of lines each of which contains fewer than 40 characters. Write a program that will center each line, using the twentieth position as the middle of the line. To wit: if a line contains 24 characters, the program should insert 8 blanks before the first character. If a line contains 11 characters, the program should insert 14 blanks before the first character.

20. Write a program that will change all occurrences of the pattern GOOD in a text file to BAD.

21. Write a program that will change all occurrences of the pattern JOHN ?. SMITH in a text file to CHARLIE BROWN, where ? stands for any character. For instance, both JOHN M. SMITH and JOHN J. SMITH should be changed to CHARLIE BROWN, while JOHN SMITH should remain intact.

22. Write a program that will search a text file for all lines containing the characters A, B, and C in columns 4, 6 and 10, respectively. The program should replace these characters in all such lines with X, Y, and Z, respectively.

23. A text file consists of telephone numbers. Each line of the file should look like this:

(???) ???-????

where ? stands for any digit, 0 through 9. Write a program that will check the validity of every line. If a line does not fit this pattern, the program should display the line number and continue on.

24. Each line of a text file consists of the year of birth of a person written as a four digit number, followed by the name of the person. Write a program that will split the file into two files. All people born before 1942 should go to the first file and all the rest should go to the second.

25. Write a program that will delete all lines of a text file that begin with a digit.

26. Write a program that will insert an empty line after each line of a given text file.

27. Write a program that will process a text file as follows. If a line consists of only two characters:

.P

then it should be replaced by an empty line and five blank characters should be inserted before the first character of the next line.

28. Text files A and B consist of the same number of lines. Each line of file A is the name of a person. The corresponding line of file B is the telephone number of the same person. Write a program that will create a new file each line of which contains both a name and the corresponding telephone number.

29. Write a program that will compute the frequency distribution of the letters in a text file.

6 Records

Let us introduce the record structure by comparing it with the array structure. Whereas an array is a collection of homogeneous components, a record's components can be heterogeneous. Whereas an array is ordinarily used to represent one attribute pertaining to several entities, such as the grades received by students in a test, a record usually represents several attributes of the same entity, such as the name, grade, age, and address of a student. Whereas the concept of arrays existed in older programming languages, such as FORTRAN, the record type is a higher-level feature that has appeared (under different names) in modern languages.

A record is characterized by its fields. The following example illustrates the way a record is introduced:

```
TYPE
   STUDENT = RECORD
                NAME : PACKED ARRAY [1..20] OF CHAR;
                GRADE : REAL;
                AGE : INTEGER;
                ADDRESS : PACKED ARRAY [1..30] OF CHAR
             END;
VAR
   SMITH, BROWN, WILSON : STUDENT;
```

Here the record type STUDENT includes the fields NAME, GRADE, AGE and AD-

DRESS. A field may itself have a structured type, such as an array or a record. In the latter case we can talk about nested records. On the other hand, a record can be an element of another structured type, such as an array or a file, in which case we can talk about an array of records or a file of records.

Just as is the case with arrays, individual components of a record are directly accessible, but they must be accessed through the use of a different notation, which is illustrated below:

```
SMITH.GRADE := 3.4;
BROWN.GRADE := 2.7;
WILSON.GRADE := 21;
WILSON.AGE := (SMITH.GRADE + BROWN.GRADE)/ 2;
IF WILSON.GRADE > 3.0
   THEN WRITE (WILSON.ADDRESS)
```

The values of all the fields of a record can be assigned to another record of the same (identical) type:

```
BROWN := WILSON
```

The WITH statement is a convenient shorthand for accessing a record's fields. The simplest form of the WITH statement is

```
WITH <record identifier>
DO <statement>
```

where the statement may use individual fields of the record as variable identifiers. A more complicated form of the WITH statement is

```
WITH A, B, C
DO <statement>
```

which is equivalent to

```
WITH A
DO WITH B
   DO WITH C
      DO <statement>
```

Sometimes a record structure depends on the value of a specific field called a tag field. For instance, a library can maintain a record for every book or journal which includes its call number, title and the year when it was published. Additionally, there can be a field indicating whether this is a book or a journal (a tag field) and if it is a book, the record can contain the author's name and the publishing house. If it is a journal, instead of the last two fields, the record can include its number. Such records are known as variant records and the syntax of a variant record type definition is shown in this example:

```
TYPE
   CATEGORY = (BOOK, JOURNAL);
   ITEM = RECORD
           CALLNUMBER : PACKED ARRAY [1..10] OF CHAR;
           TITLE : PACKED ARRAY [1..30] OF CHAR;
           YEAR : INTEGER;
           CASE KIND : CATEGORY OF
               BOOK : (AUTHOR : PACKED ARRAY [1..20] OF CHAR;
                       PUBLISHER : PACKED ARRAY [1..
                       15] OF CHAR);
               JOURNAL : (NUMBER : INTEGER)
           END;
```

The fixed part (CALLNUMBER, TITLE and YEAR in our example) always precedes the variant part. A record can have only one variant part, although variant parts can be nested. If no variant fields are associated with a value of the tag field, an empty field list must be given:

```
A = RECORD
        B : C;
        CASE D : E OF
           F : (G, H : I);
           J : ()
        END;
```

The tag field can be omitted but the tag field type must be present (it is an ordinal type). The tag values must always agree with the tag field type.

DEFINITIONS AND DECLARATIONS

1. Declare a record that will organize the following data items: month, day, year.

2. Three record types have been defined:

```
TYPE
    PERSON1 = RECORD
                  ID : INTEGER;
                  SALARY : REAL;
                  SENIORITY : INTEGER
              END;
    PERSON2 = RECORD
                  ID : INTEGER;
                  AGE : INTEGER;
                  SALARY : REAL
              END;
```

```
PERSON3 = RECORD
               ID : INTEGER;
               ID : CHAR;
               SEX : CHAR
         END;
```

Are these definitions valid?

3. There are 30 students in a class and the following information is recorded for each student: name, year of birth, the number of units taken, and GPA. Declare a variable describing this information.

4. A professor teaches three classes and maintains a list of student names for each class. Declare a variable capable of storing this information.

5. A hospital maintains the following information about each patient: name, room number, morning condition and afternoon condition where both morning and afternoon conditions consist of the patient's temperature and blood pressure. Define a data structure modeling this information.

6. Find and correct the error in the following definition:

```
TYPE
   A = RECORD
            A1 : INTEGER;
            A2 : REAL;
            A3 : B
         END;
   B = RECORD
            B1 : CHAR;
            B2 : REAL
         END;
```

7. Redeclare the variable BOOK without explicitly defining its type.

```
TYPE
   STRING = PACKED ARRAY [1..30] OF CHAR;
   CATEGORY = (FICTION, BIOGRAPHY, TEXTBOOK, MANUAL);
   BOOKTYPE = RECORD
                 AUTHOR : STRING;
                 TITLE : STRING;
                 GROUP : CATEGORY;
                 PRICE : REAL
              END;
VAR
   BOOK : BOOKTYPE;
```

8. Are the following declarations valid?

```
VAR
   X : REAL;
   Y : RECORD
           X : INTEGER;
           Y : CHAR;
           Z : RECORD
                   Y : REAL;
                   Z : BOOLEAN
               END
       END;
```

9. May a record have only one field?

10. May a field identifier be the same as

   a. a constant identifier
   b. a function identifier
   c. a record identifier
   d. a type identifier?

11. May a record identifier be a parameter of a function or a procedure?

12. The variable X is declared below thrice:

   a. TYPE
         A = RECORD
                 B : INTEGER;
                 C : CHAR;
                 D : INTEGER
             END;
      VAR
         X : A;

   b. TYPE
         A = RECORD
                 B : INTEGER;
                 D : INTEGER;
                 C : CHAR
             END;
      VAR
         X : A;

   c. TYPE
         A = RECORD
                 B, D : INTEGER;
                 C : CHAR
```
```

```
          END;
     VAR
        X : A;
```

Are these declarations equivalent?

13. CLIENT is a record variable. Comment on this statement:

```
WRITE (CLIENT)
```

ACCESS METHODS

1. Assign some values to all fields of the record declared below:

```
TYPE
   HOUSE = RECORD
             NUMBEROFROOMS : INTEGER;
             ADDRESS : RECORD
                         STREETADDRESS : PACKED ARRAY
                         [1..30] OF CHAR;
                         CITY : PACKED ARRAY [1..15] OF
                                CHAR
                       END;
             PRICE : REAL
           END;
VAR
   MYHOUSE : HOUSE;
```

2. Consider this declaration:

```
TYPE
   A = RECORD
          B : INTEGER;
          C : CHAR;
          D : REAL
       END;
   E = ARRAY ['X'..'Z'] OF A;
VAR
   F : E;
```

How do you access individual fields of F?

3. Use the WITH statement to assign some values to all fields of the record BOOK declared in problem 7 in the previous section.

4. Use the WITH statement to assign some values to all fields of the record MYHOUSE declared in problem 1.

5. Use the WITH statement to assign some values to all fields of the array of records F declared in problem 2.

6. Must A and B be nested records in this structure:

```
WITH A, B
DO <statement>
```

Give appropriate examples.

7. May the constructions

```
WITH A, B
DO <statement>
```

and

```
WITH B, A
DO <statement>
```

be equivalent?

8. The records HOUSE1 and HOUSE 2 are not nested. Both records include the field PRICE. What will happen if this statement

```
WITH HOUSE1, HOUSE2
DO IF PRICE < 100000
        THEN WRITE ('THIS HOUSE IS AFFORDABLE')
```

appears in the program?

9. Explain the difference between

```
BOOK [5].AUTHOR
```

and

```
BOOK.AUTHOR [5]
```

10. The following definitions and declarations have been made:

```
TYPE
   A = RECORD
           X : INTEGER;
           Y : CHAR
       END;
   B = RECORD
           X : INTEGER;
           Y : CHAR
       END;
VAR
   M, N : A;
   P : B;
```

Which of the statements below are legal?

a. M := N
b. M := P
c. P := N

11. Write a program that will solicit and read student records. Each record consists of a student's ID and GPA. The program will store all records and then will print those in which GPA is above a given number.

12. Each line of a text text file contains the following information about a student: name, GPA, the number of units taken, and the number of years in college. Write a program that will print the highest GPA achieved among the students who have taken more than 30 units and who are in their fourth year in college or who have taken more than 25 units and are in their third year in college.

VARIANT RECORDS

1. Define a record suitable for storing the following information about a bank account. Each account has a number, the customer's name, and a balance. It can be either a savings account or a checking account. In the former case, the only additional recorded piece of information is an interest rate. In the latter case, the account may or may not have overdraft protection, and the balance may or may not have dropped below $500 during the current month, which determines whether or not any interest will be credited in the end of the month.

Find the error in each of the following definitions (2-8).

2.
```
TYPE
    A = (B, C);
    D = RECORD
            E : REAL;
            CASE F : A OF
                B : (G, H : 1..10);
                C : (I : CHAR)
            END;
            J : INTEGER
        END;
```

3.
```
TYPE
    H = (I, L);
    M = (N, O);
    A = RECORD
            B : -10..10;
            C : (D, E, F);
            CASE G : H OF
                I : (J, K : CHAR);
```

```
            L : ()
        CASE M OF
            N : ();
            O : (P : REAL; Q : BOOLEAN)
    END;
```

4. TYPE
```
    A = RECORD
            CASE A : B OF
                C : (X, Y, Z : INTEGER);
                D : (X : INTEGER)
        END;
```

5. TYPE
```
    A = RECORD
            CASE B : REAL OF
                1.5 : (C, D : INTEGER);
                1.6 : (E : CHAR)
        END;
```

6. TYPE
```
    A = RECORD
            CASE B : CHAR OF
                1 : (C, D : INTEGER);
                2 : ()
        END;
```

7. TYPE
```
    A = (B, C);
    D = RECORD
            CASE E : A OF
                B : (F : CHAR);
                C : ();
                B : (G, H : CHAR)
        END;
```

8. TYPE
```
    A = (B, C, D);
    E = (F, G, H);
    I = RECORD
            CASE J : E OF
                B : ();
                C : (K, L : A);
                D : (M : A)
        END;
```

9. Comment on these definitions:

   a. **A = RECORD**
          CASE B : C OF
          . . . .
         END;

   b. **A = RECORD**
          CASE B OF
          . . . .
         END;

   c. **A = RECORD**
          CASE OF
         . . . .
         END;

10. A record with nested variant parts, PERSON1, is defined as follows:

```
TYPE
    STRING = PACKED ARRAY [1..10] OF CHAR;
    STATUS = (SINGLE, MARRIED, SEPARATED);
    PERSON = RECORD
                NAME : STRING;
                AGE : INTEGER;
                CASE MARSTATUS : STATUS OF
                    SINGLE : ();
                    MARRIED : (SPOUSENAME : STRING;
                                    CASE DEPENDENTS : BOOLEAN OF
                                        TRUE : (NUMBER : INTEGER);
                                        FALSE : ());
                    SEPARATED : (YEAR : INTEGER)
            END;
VAR
    PERSON1 : PERSON;
```

Give several examples of assignments to all fields of the record.

11. The list of field declarations for all values of the constants is empty:

```
        TYPE
            A = 1..3;
            B = RECORD
                    . . . . . . . . . . . .
                    CASE C : A OF
```

```
                1 : ( );
                2 : ( );
                3 : ( )
        END;
```

What can you say about this record?

12. A record is defined as follows:

```
    TYPE
        A = (X, Y, Z);
        B = RECORD
                . . . . . . . . . . . . .
                CASE C : A OF
                    X : (M, N : REAL);
                    Y : (P, Q : CHAR);
                    Z : ( )
            END;
    VAR
        H : B;
```

and this assignment is made:

```
    H.C := X;
```

What will happen if the next statement is

```
    H.P := 'S'
```

13. Use the WITH and CASE statements to provide an error-prone access scheme to the fields of the record H declared in the previous problem.

14. Each line of a text file contains the following information about an employee: name, ID, sex, salary, and whether or not he or she is a union member. If he or she is a member, it also includes the name of the union representing the employee. Write a program that will split the file into two: one for the unionized members and the other for the nonunionized ones. The former file should include the names, IDs, and union names, while the latter should include the names, IDs, and salaries.

7 Pointers and Their Applications

A pointer is a variable whose value is the address of another variable. Pointers can be declared as follows.

```
TYPE
    TYPEOFCHARPOINTER = ^CHAR;
    TYPEOFREALPOINTER = ^REAL;
VAR
    CHARPOINTER : TYPEOFCHARPOINTER;
    REALPOINTER : TYPEOFREALPOINTER;
```

The variables referenced by pointers are called *dynamic variables*. They are anonymous and are denoted by the pointer's name followed by an up-arrow or caret, as in

```
CHARPOINTER ^
REALPOINTER ^
```

A call to the standard procedure NEW creates such a variable and assigns its address to its pointer. After the call

```
NEW (CHARPOINTER)
```

the variable CHARPOINTER ^ is created but not initialized yet. The address of

CHARPOINTER^ is assigned to CHARPOINTER. A call to the standard procedure DISPOSE, whose argument is a pointer variable, deletes the variable referenced by the pointer, and the value of the pointer becomes undefined.

If the value NIL assigned to a pointer of any type, the pointer does not point to any memory location. The value of a pointer can be assigned to another pointer of the same type. Two pointers can be compared with the operators = (equal) and < > (not equal).

Pointers are most often used in building linked structures. Let us consider the following declarations.

```
TYPE
    ENTITYPOINTER = ^ENTITY;
    ENTITY = RECORD
                ID : INTEGER;
                NEXTPOINTER : ENTITYPOINTER
            END;
VAR
    START : ENTITYPOINTER;
```

The call

```
NEW (START)
```

creates a record START^ with the fields START^. ID and START^. NEXTPOINTER. This record can be initialized, for example, as follows:

```
START^.ID := 10;
NEW (START^.NEXTPOINTER )
```

These statements create a new record

```
START^.NEXTPOINTER^
```

with the fields

```
START^.NEXTPOINTER^.ID
```

and

```
START^.NEXTPOINTER^.NEXTPOINTER
```

This example shows a way to build a simple linked list in Pascal. The links in the list are records. Each record includes both the information field (or fields) and the pointer field (or fields) linking it with another record (or records).

THE NOTION OF A POINTER

1. The value of a pointer variable

a. Has the same type as the variable it points to
b. Is the address of a memory location
c. Can be inspected with a WRITE statement
d. Can be incremented but not decremented

Comment on these statements.

2. A dynamic variable

a. Is a variable of the pointer type
b. Cannot be a Boolean variable
c. Can be created and deleted by statements in the program
d. Is a component of a linked data structure

3. Comment on these statements:

a. The variable referenced by a pointer can be inspected with a WRITE statement.
b. The variable referenced by a pointer can be both on the left and right sides of an assignment statement.
c. The name of the variable referenced by a pointer is independent of the pointer's name.
d. Any assignment to a pointer affects the value of the variable referenced by the pointer.

Find the error in each of the following program segments (4-13).

4. ```
TYPE
     TYPEOFCHARPOINTER = ^CHAR;
VAR
     CHARPOINTER : TYPEOFCHARPOINTER;
BEGIN
     CHARPOINTER^ := 'A';
```

5. ```
TYPE
     TYPEOFCHARPOINTER = ^CHAR;
VAR
     CHARPOINTER : TYPEOFCHARPOINTER;
BEGIN
     NEW (CHARPOINTER);
     IF ORD (CHARPOINTER^) > 10
          THEN WRITELN ('WATCH OUT')
```

6. ```
TYPE
     TYPEOFREALPOINTER = ^REAL;
VAR
     ONE, TWO : TYPEOFREALPOINTER;
```
```

```
    BEGIN
        NEW (ONE);
        TWO := ONE + 8;

 7. TYPE
        TYPEOFREALPOINTER = ^REAL;
    VAR
        REALPOINTER : TYPEOFREALPOINTER;
    BEGIN
        NEW (REALPOINTER);
        REALPOINTER^ := NIL;


 8. TYPE
        TYPEOFBOOLEANPOINTER = ^BOOLEAN;
    VAR
        BOOLEANPOINTER : TYPEOFBOOLEANPOINTER;
    BEGIN
        NEW (BOOLEANPOINTER);
        BOOLEANPOINTER^ := TRUE;
        DISPOSE (BOOLEANPOINTER);
        IF NOT BOOLEANPOINTER^
            THEN WRITE ('BE CAREFUL')


 9. TYPE
        TYPEOFCHARPOINTER = ^CHAR;
    VAR
        CHARPOINTER : TYPEOFCHARPOINTER;
    BEGIN
        NEW (CHARPOINTER);
        CHARPOINTER := NIL;
        CHARPOINTER^ := 'X';


10. TYPE
        TYPEOFINTEGERPOINTER = ^INTEGER;
        TYPEOFREALPOINTER = ^REAL;
    VAR
        INTEGERPOINTER : TYPEOFINTEGERPOINTER;
        REALPOINTER : TYPEOFREALPOINTER;
    BEGIN
        NEW (INTEGERPOINTER);
        REALPOINTER := INTEGERPOINTER;


11. TYPE
        TYPEOFCHARPOINTER = ^CHAR;
    VAR
```

```
        CHARPOINTER : TYPEOFCHARPOINTER;
    BEGIN
        NEW (CHARPOINTER);
        WRITE (CHARPOINTER);
```

12.
```
    TYPE
        TYPEOFREALPOINTER = ^REAL;
    VAR
        ONE, TWO : TYPEOFREALPOINTER;
    BEGIN
        NEW (ONE);
        NEW (TWO);
        ONE^ := 1.0;
        TWO^ := 2.0;
        IF ONE <= TWO
            THEN WRITE ('ONE IS LESS THAN TWO');
```

13.
```
    TYPE
        NODE = RECORD
                    NAME : INTEGER;
                    LEFT : NODEPOINTER;
                    RIGHT : NODEPOINTER
                END;
        NODEPOINTER = ^NODE;
```

14. NUMBER is a variable declared in a program. How do you make a pointer point to NUMBER?

15. May a pointer be passed as a parameter to a procedure or a function?

16. May a function have the pointer type?

17. P is a pointer to a real variable; Q is a pointer to an integer variable. Are the following statements valid?

```
    READ (P^);
    WRITE (Q^)
```

18. Explain the difference between the two statements:

```
    P := Q
```

and

```
    P^ := Q^
```

(assuming that all necessary allocations and initializations have been made).

19. May several pointers point to the same dynamic variable?

20. P is declared as a pointer to a real variable. Q is declared as a pointer to an integer variable. The value NIL is assigned to P. May NIL be assigned to Q as well?

21. The following statements have been executed:

```
NEW (P);
Q := P;
P^ := 5;
DISPOSE (Q)
```

Can P^ be accessed at this point?

22. The following statements have been executed:

```
NEW (P);
NEW (Q);
P^ := 5;
P := Q
```

What is the value of P^ at this point?

LINKED STRUCTURES

1. Write a program that will read social security numbers from a text file and create a linked list of the numbers in the order they appear in the file.

2. Using the notations of the previous problem, write a program segment that will compute the number of records in a linked list.

3. A linked list looks like this:

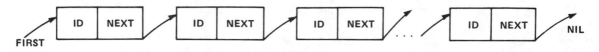

FIRST

Suppose that the ID field of each record is an integer number and the list has been sorted according to the ascending order of the record IDs. Write a program segment that will insert a new record in the proper place.

4. Change this linked list

FIRST

RECORD 1   RECORD 2   RECORD 3   RECORD 4   RECORD 5

90

to this

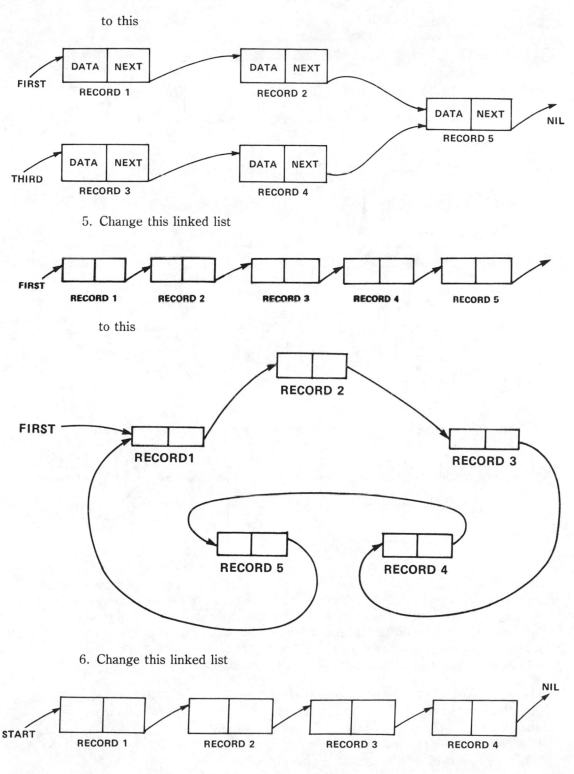

5. Change this linked list

to this

6. Change this linked list

to this

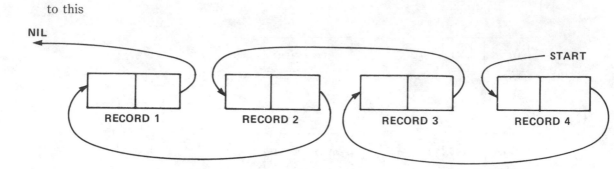

7. Merge these two linked lists

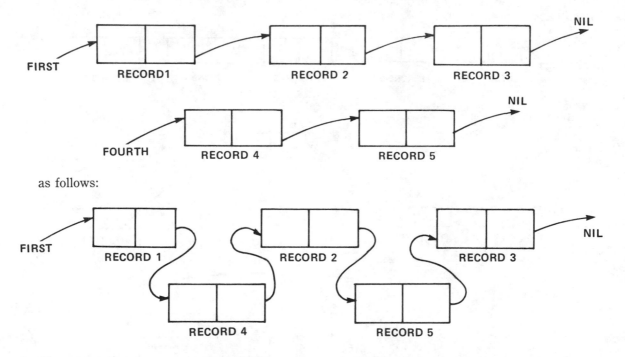

as follows:

8. Dynamic variables are stored in a stack-like structure called the heap. Some Pascal implementations ignore calls for DISPOSE and do not bother to remove unneeded records, in which case the heap may soon become exhausted. One of several methods of storage reclamation is called garbage collection. This method is based on determining which records are still in use, marking them and removing unmarked ones. Try to think up a simple garbage collection algorithm.

9. There are two linked lists of records. Each record has two fields: ID and pointer. The IDs are strings and both lists have been sorted according to the lexicographic order of the IDs. Write a program that will merge the two lists, so that the resulting list will be sorted lexicographically as well.

10. Suppose that each record has two pointer fields, one pointing to the preceding record and one to the following record. Such a data structure is called a doubly-linked list. A doubly-linked list is depicted in the following figure.

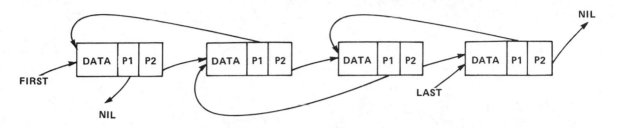

Write a program that will create a doubly-linked list depicted in this figure.

11. A binary plex is a data structure resembling a genealogical tree. Each record of such a structure includes two pointer fields, but some pointers may equal NIL. An example of a binary plex is depicted in the figure below.

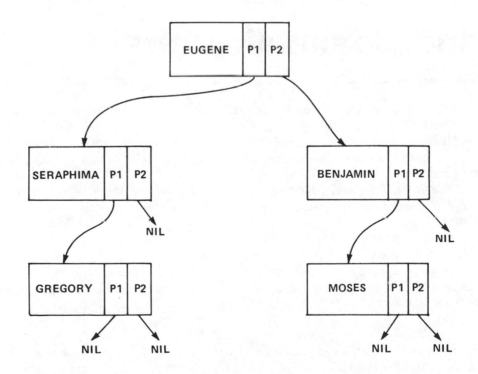

Write a program that will create the depicted binary plex.

12. Consider a general binary plex of the type described in the previous problem. Try to think up an algorithm searching for a given name among all records making up the plex.

8 Style, Efficiency and Common Errors

This chapter, unlike the others, does not introduce new Pascal concepts but rather deals with general principles applicable to programming as a whole. Since the subject of this chapter is open-ended, I have chosen not to precede it by a coherent introduction. Instead, I have enumerated some important pieces of advice or caution to the reader, fully realizing that my choices are subjective.

The order of the advice has no significance whatsoever. The problems following this introduction can be divided into two groups. The problems in the first group illustrate specific points, and they are solved in Part 2. The problems in the second group are intended to serve as food for thought. They are real life problems taken from such diverse fields as data processing, Monte Carlo simulation, and mathematical statistics, which can be used as more challenging projects. Here you have a chance to apply the material in this and all preceding chapters. Since, as a rule, there are many solutions to these problems, I have provided only very laconic, if any, comments on them.

1. The layout of a program is important. It can enhance the readability of the program, and in general, can make it look more appealing. Quite a few different layout conventions have been proposed by different authors and the choice of the layout for your program is a matter of taste. Here are some good examples of indentation standards.

- For definition and declarations:

```
CONST
   MAX = 10;
TYPE
   LISTTYPE = ARRAY [1..MAX] OF REAL;
VAR
   LIST : LISTTYPE;
```

- For compound statements:

```
BEGIN
   <statement 1>;
   <statement 2>;
   . . . . . . . . . . . .
   <statement n>
END
```

- For IF statements:

```
IF <Boolean expression>
   THEN <statement 1>
   ELSE <statement 2>
```

Matching BEGINs and ENDs should always be aligned. Avoid saving space by crowding language elements. For example, this statement

```
X := Y + Z
```

looks much prettier than

```
X:=Y+Z
```

It is not a good idea to put several statements on one line. Various sections of a program should be separated by blank lines or by other means, such as

```
(****************************************************
*                                                  *
*      THIS IS THE BEGINNING OF THE NEXT           *
*      SECTION OF THIS PROGRAM THAT VERIFIES        *
*      THE INPUT DATA                              *
*                                                  *
****************************************************)
```

If labels are used at all, use a generous numbering scheme. To wit, use 100, 110, 120 in one program section and 200, 210, 220 in another.

There are programs that format Pascal programs, or in other words, produce neatly arranged programs out of arbitrarily written but syntactically correct ones.

2. Programs should be adequately commented. The comments should not repeat the code. For example, the comment in this program segment

```
{THE FOLLOWING LOOP STATEMENT EXECUTES STATEMENT
 S FOR ALL VALUES OF I RANGING FROM 1 THROUGH 10 }
FOR I := 1 TO 10
DO S
```

does not clarify anything.

3. Meaningful identifiers make a program self-documenting.

4. The design of large programs should normally proceed in a top-down fashion. This means that the entire program is broken into smaller problems which, in turn, are broken into still smaller problems, and so on. This process of decomposition or successive refinement is repeated until the resulting subproblems are easy to express in Pascal.

It is natural to implement the subproblems as procedures and functions. The main program should be simple and consist of procedure and function calls.

5. The use of constants makes a program more modifiable. Thus, even though it may be assumed that the employees' names will be adequately represented by strings that are 20 characters long, it is still a good idea to define a constant equal to 20 and then use it instead of the number 20. Should the need to modify this parameter arise in the future, it will be much easier to change the value of one constant than to look for all its occurrences.

6. Pascal provides several control structures, and oftentimes there are several ways to encode a program segment; however, this built-in redundancy of the language is illusory. Usually, there is a control structure that is adequate for a given problem, while the use of the other structures would be unnatural.

The same holds true for data structures. Thus, in a situation where some data can be represented either as a group of arrays or as one array of records, the "right" choice depends on the essence of the problem, and the use of the "right" data structure can help clarify the problem.

7. Usually a program is based on certain assumptions about the input data. These assumptions should be verified by the program to the greatest extent possible and practicable.

8. It is much easier to debug, analyze and validate a large program if it is broken into small manageable procedures and functions. A powerful way to increase the independence and usefulness of these smaller units is the utilization of parameters as a means of communication between the units.

9. A program is said to be portable if it can run on different computers. If a program uses nonstandard features of a specific implementation, it may not be portable. Hence, the programmer should always be aware of the trade-off between efficiency and portability.

10. Another important trade-off is that between efficiency and simplicity. Program A is said to be more efficient than program B if both produce the same results, but A either runs faster, consists of fewer statements, or requires less memory. Thus, program segment 2 below is more efficient than program segment 1, and program segment 3 is more efficient than program segment 2.

```
1. SUM := 0;
   FOR COUNTER := FIRST TO LAST
   DO BEGIN
         SUM := SUM + ELEMENT [COUNTER];
         Z := 0
   END;
   SUMOFSQUARES := 0;
   FOR COUNTER := FIRST TO LAST
   DO SUMOFSQUARES := SUMOFSQUARES + SQR (ELEMENT
                                  [COUNTER])

2. SUM := 0;
   Z := 0;
   FOR COUNTER := FIRST TO LAST
   DO SUM := SUM + ELEMENT [COUNTER];
   SUMOFSQUARES := 0;
   FOR COUNTER := FIRST TO LAST
   DO SUMOFSQUARES := SUMOFSQUARES + SQR (ELEMENT
                                  [COUNTER])

3. SUM := 0;
   SUMOFSQUARES :=0;
   Z :=0;
   FOR COUNTER := FIRST TO LAST
   DO BEGIN
         SUM := SUM + ELEMENT [COUNTER];
         SUMOFSQUARES := SUMOFSQUARES + SQR
                             (ELEMENT [COUNTER])
   END
```

The improvements made in the foregoing example are obvious. They make the code more efficient without sacrificing its simplicity. But if a program is made more efficient at the expense of simplicity, the change may or may not be worth it. Note that some Pascal compilers make simple improvements, such as moving constants out of loops automatically.

PROBLEMS

1. The layout of the following program segment is misleading.

```
IF <condition 1>
    THEN IF <condition 2>
            THEN <statement 1>
    ELSE <statement 2>
```

Correct it.

2. Make the following program segment more efficient.

```
SUM := 0.0;
FOR COUNTER := FIRST TO LAST
DO SUM := SUM + 2.7 * EXP (-3.1) * X [COUNTER]
```

3. Improve the efficiency of the following program segment.

```
IF <condition 1>
    THEN IF <condition 2>
            THEN <statement 1>
            ELSE <statement 2>
    ELSE <statement 2>
```

4. Simplify the following structure.

```
        FOR COUNTER := FIRST TO LAST
        DO BEGIN
                <statement 1>;
                IF <condition>
                    THEN GOTO 10
            END;
10 : <statement 2>
```

5. Simplify the following structure.

```
COUNTER := FIRST;
WHILE COUNTER <= LAST
DO BEGIN
        <statement>;
        COUNTER := COUNTER + 1
    END
```

6. The array GRADES has been declared as follows:

```
TYPE
    TYPEOFGRADES = ARRAY [1..30] OF INTEGER;
VAR
    GRADES : TYPEOFGRADES;
```

Find the flaw in this program segment:

```
WRITELN ('PLEASE, ENTER THE NUMBER OF GRADES');
READLN (NUMBER);
FOR COUNTER := 1 TO NUMBER
DO BEGIN
    WRITELN ('PLEASE, ENTER GRADE NUMBER ',COUNTER);
    READLN (GRADES [COUNTER])
END
```

7. The following program segment should compute the sum $0.1 + 0.2 + 0.3 + \ldots + 99.9$. It contains a flaw. Find it and correct it.

```
SUM := 0.0;
I := 0.1;
WHILE I <> 100.0
DO BEGIN
    SUM := SUM + I;
    I := I + 0.1
END
```

8. The top-down design is

   a. A way to write error-free programs
   b. A method of design based on decomposition of large problems into small ones
   c. A method of documenting programs based on flowcharts
      Choose the right answer.

9. Which of the statements below are correct and which are not?

   a. Comments should not provide any new information in addition to what is already conveyed by the code.
   b. Comments should not be interspersed with the code.
   c. Comments should make up 50% of a program.
   d. Comments can be useful to the author of a program as well as to other people who will read the program.
   e. Comments slow down the program execution.

10. Comment on this statement: a well-written procedure can be used by several programs.

11. There is a wide class of programs that use pseudorandom numbers. Pseudorandom numbers are generated by programs and therefore are not quite random. However, good programs generate sequences that behave almost like random numbers. Many of such programs are based on an idea proposed by D. H. Lehmer in 1948. A sequence of pseudorandom numbers, called a linear congruent sequence, can be obtained iteratively as follows:

```
X [N] := (A * X [N - 1] + B) MOD C;
Y [N] := X [N] / C
```

Here A, B and C are integer constants, X [N] is a sequence of integer numbers and Y [N] is a sequence of real numbers between 0.0 and 1.0. If A, B and C are chosen well, the sequence Y [N] behaves almost like random numbers uniformly distributed between 0 and 1. X [1] can be chosen arbitrarily and it is called the seed. Sooner or later X [N] will be equal to X [1], after which the entire sequence will repeat; but for well-chosen A's, B's, and C's, the period can be very long. Unfortunately, the choice of A, B, and C is computer dependent, and although there are some theoretical guidelines as to how to choose them, this is essentially an empirical problem.

Needless to say that in most cases only one member of the sequence of pseudorandom numbers should be stored. When it is necessary to generate a new number, it is stored in the same location.

To generate a sequence of pseudorandom numbers with an arbitrary distribution function F (t), you have to solve this equation

```
Y [N] = F ( T [N])
```

with respect to T [N], where Y [N] are numbers uniformly distributed between 0 and 1.

Write a program to generate pseudorandom numbers uniformly distributed between
    0 and 1;
  −1 and 1;
  10 and 30.

12. Use pseudorandom numbers to simulate the tossing of a coin.

13. Use pseudorandom numbers to simulate the tossing of a die.

14. Write a program that will use pseudorandom numbers to play tic-tac-toe with the user.

15. Compute the number pi using pseudorandom numbers.

16. The Geiger-Muller counter is a radiation detector. It counts the number of events

produced by the passage of particles. However, there is an error associated with each Geiger-Muller counter caused by the following fact. After the passage of a particle produces a discharge that is detected by the counter, there is a short but significant dead time during which the detector does not respond to new particles.

Write a program that will determine the accuracy of the counter or the ratio of the number of detected particles to the total number. Assume that the interval between two successive particles is a random variable with a given distribution function and the dead time is a random variable with another distribution function.

17. Let us modify the previous problem. Suppose that any particle appearing during a dead time goes undetected, but it extends the current dead time. Write a program that will simulate the Geiger-Muller counter with this modification.

18. Sorting is the rearrangement of some items into ascending or descending order. For the sake of simplicity, let us talk about sorting of an array of numbers.

A well known sorting method is called *sorting by insertion*. I will define this method of sorting recursively. Assume that the first K elements of the array have already been sorted. Then insert the $(K+1)$-st element in the proper location among the previously sorted elements, moving some of them if necessary.

There are several versions of this type of sorting. Write a program implementing the simplest one. Assume that the elements are rearranged into ascending order. The new element is compared with the largest among those already sorted, then with the second largest, and so on, until the first number smaller than the new one is found. Then all the larger numbers are moved up one space while the new one is inserted.

19. The bubble sort method of sorting can be described as follows. Element 1 is compared with element 2 and the two are interchanged if necessary. Then the (new) element 2 is compared with element 3 and they are interchanged if necessary. At the end of the first pass, do the same to the next-to-last and last elements. Then begin the second pass, and so on. The algorithm terminates when there have been no interchanges during an entire pass. Write a program implementing this algorithm.

20. There are two sorted arrays and you want to merge them or to create a new sorted array whose elements are all elements of the two original arrays. Invent a simple algorithm accomplishing this, and write a program implementing the algorithm.

21. The following test, known as the Wilcoxon test, is used in mathematical statistics to verify the hypothesis that two samples come from identical populations. Here is how it works.

Suppose that the first sample consists of M numbers:

```
X [1], X [2],..., X [M]
```

and the second sample consists of N numbers:

$$Y [1], Y [2], ..., Y [N].$$

First merge the two arrays and rearrange them into ascending order (but still keep track of which array each number comes from). Then compute the sum of the ranks occupied by all elements of the first array and by all elements of the second array. For example, if the original arrays are

13.4 17.8 11.6 9.12 6.34

and 8.66 12.4 14.5

the combined rearranged array is

6.34 8.66 9.12 11.6 12.4 13.4 14.5 17.8

and the ranks are

6 8 4 3 1

and 2 5 7

for array 1 and array 2, respectively. The sums of the ranks are 22 and 14, respectively.

Next compute U according to this formula:

$$U = M * N + M * (M + 1) / 2 - R1,$$

where R1 is the sum of the ranks of the first array. In this example U = 15 + 15 − 22 = 8.

Finally, the hypothesis (that the two samples or arrays come from identical populations) is rejected if the absolute value of Z is greater than a fixed number, say 1.96, where

$$Z = (U - \text{EXPECTATION } (U)) / \text{STANDARD DEVIATION } (U),$$

where

$$\text{EXPECTATION } (U) = M * N / 2$$

and

$$\text{STANDARD DEVIATION } (U) = \text{SQRT } (M * N * (M + N + 1) / 12)$$

Write a program implementing this algorithm.

9 VAX-11 Pascal

VAX-11 Pascal is an implementation of the Pascal language that has been developed to run under the VAX/VMS operating system created by Digital Equipment Corporation. It includes numerous extensions of standard Pascal. Here is a brief summary of main extensions and additional capabilities, as well as some definitions of elements that are left undefined in standard Pascal.

1. The character set includes both uppercase and lowercase letters. However, the compiler is case insensitive with one exception, namely, when letters appear between single quotes. The following special characters are included in the character set:

!	exclamation mark	;	semicolon
"	double quote	<	less than
#	number sign	=	equal sign
$	dollar sign	>	greater than
%	percent sign	?	question mark
&	ampersand	@	at sign
'	single quote	\	back slash
(	left parenthesis	]	right square bracket
)	right parenthesis	^	up arrow
*	asterisk	_	underscore
+	plus sign	`	reverse single quote
,	comma	{	left curly bracket

–	minus sign	|	vertical line
.	period	}	right curly bracket
/	slash	~	tilde
:	colon		

2. In addition to the standard reserved words, the following words are reserved in VAX-11 Pascal:

%DESCR	MODULE
%IMMED	OTHERWISE
%INCLUDE	REM
%REF	VALUE
%STDESCR	VARYING

3. The compiler remembers the first 31 characters of an identifier. To enhance the readability of a program, underscore characters can be included in identifiers.

4. The command %INCLUDE <file> inserts the content of the given file right at the point where the %INCLUDE statement is located.

5. There are several extra data types: DOUBLE-precision reals, QUADRUPLE-precision reals, UNSIGNED integers, VARYING OF CHAR strings.

6. In VAX-11 Pascal, version 2, the MOD operator is defined only if the second operand is positive. There is another operator, REM, which also operates on integer operands and computes the remainder from the DIV operation. Either operand of REM can be negative.

7. A special exponentiation operator, **, is provided, the order of precedence being the same as in mathematics.

8. The range of INTEGER numbers is from $-(2 ** 31 - 1)$ to $2 ** 31 - 1$. The range of REAL numbers is from $-1.7 * 10 ** 38$ to $1.7 * 10 ** 38$. The range of QUADRUPLE-precision numbers is from $-0.59 * 10 ** 4932$ to $0.59 * 10 ** 4932$.
  The smallest positive REAL number is $0.29 * 10 ** (-38)$. The smallest positive QUADRUPLE-precision number is $0.84 * 10 ** (-4932)$.

9. Integers can be specified in binary, octal and hexadecimal notations.

10. A SET of INTEGER numbers may not have more than 256 elements. Moreover, it may include only numbers from 0 to 255.

11. The maximum number of values that can be taken by a variable of a user-defined ordinal type is 63,535.

12. The label declaration part, the constant definition part, the type definition part, the variable declaration part, and the procedure and function declaration part may appear in any order, and each of them may appear more than once. It is legal, for example, to redefine a constant in a constant definition part; however, it is illegal, for example, to use a type identifier in other definitions before it itself has been defined.

13. Variables, including structured ones, may be initialized in the variable declaration part. Thus, these declarations are legal.

```
VAR A, B, C : REAL := 0.0;
    COLOR_HAIR : HAIR_COLOR := (LIGHT, DARK, RED);
```

14. The CASE statement can include the OTHERWISE clause. If it is included, it specifies the statement to be executed if the value of the CASE expression is not in the constant list.

15. There are many additional standard functions and procedures. Here are just a few examples.

- DBLE (X) - converts the value of X to the double-precision form.
- SNGL (X) - converts the value of X to the single-precision form.
- INDEX (STR, PATTERN) - searches for the first occurrence of the pattern within the string. The function returns an integer value indicating the position of the pattern in the string. If the pattern is not found, the function returns 0.
- LENGTH (STR) - returns the length of a string as an integer value.
- SUBSTR (STR, START, LENGTH) - returns a substring of a string.
- CARD (S) - returns the number of elements in the set expression S.
- DATE (STR) - assigns the current date to a string.
- TIME (STR) - assigns the current time to a string.

16. Additional input and output capabilities can be specified by the OPEN and CLOSE procedures.

17. There are attributes that instruct the compiler to change its rules in some ways.

The main reference used by the author for writing this chapter was "VAX-11 Pascal Reference Manual (Version V2.0)" published by DEC in October, 1982. This chapter is by no means intended to replace the Reference Manual but rather to give you the flavor of a real-life implementation and to help introduce you to one of the most common implementations of Pascal.

I had to be very selective, because the Reference Manual provides such a wealth of material that it cannot be covered in one chapter. Most of the subjects that turned out to be beyond the scope of this chapter are those that are heavily dependent on concepts foreign to Pascal, such as VAX-11 Record Management Services and options of the compiler.

PROBLEMS

1. Is this declaration part valid in VAX-11 Pascal?

```
VAR
    NUMBER_OF_PARTS : INTEGER;
    number_of_parts : integer;
```

2. What will be printed after execution of these statements?

```
a. WRITELN ('HELLO')
b. WRITELN ('hello')
c. writeln ('HELLO')
d. writeln ('hello')
e. Writeln ('Hello')
f. WRITELN ('HELLo')
```

3. In an ASCII table, find the values of

```
a. ORD ('R')
b. ORD ('r')
c. ORD ('5')
d. ORD (5)
e. ORD ('?')
f. ORD ('+')
```

4. How do you specify the argument of the WRITELN statement if you want to have a character printed and underlined?

5. Rewrite the program MYSTERY without using %INCLUDE directives.

```
PROGRAM MYSTERY ...
    .
    .
    .
BEGIN
    %INCLUDE 'FIRST.PAS'
    .
    .
```

```
        •
    %INCLUDE 'LAST.PAS'
  END.
```

where the file FIRST.PAS is

```
    WRITELN ('HELLO');
    WRITELN ('WE ARE BEGINNING OUR PROGRAM NOW');
```

and the file LAST.PAS is

```
    WRITELN ('GOOD-BYE');
    WRITELN ('IT WAS NICE WORKING WITH YOU')
```

6. Is the following construction legal?

```
    PROGRAM ABC ...
            •
            •
            •
        %INCLUDE KLM.PAS
            •
            •
            •
    END.
```

where the file KLM.PAS is

```
        •
        •
        •
    %INCLUDE PQR.PAS
        •
        •
        •
```

where the file PQR.PAS is

```
        •
        •
        •
    %INCLUDE XYZ.PAS
        •
        •
        •
```

etc.

7. Is the following construction legal?

```
PROGRAM ABC ...
        .
        .
        .
    %INCLUDE KLM.PAS
        .
        .
        .
END.
```

where the file KLM.PAS is

```
    .
    .
    .
%INCLUDE PQR.PAS
    .
    .
    .
```

where the file PQR.PAS is

```
    .
    .
    .
%INCLUDE ABC.PAS
    .
    .
    .
```

where the file ABC.PAS is the file containing the program ABC.

8. Rewrite the following assignment statement using binary, octal and hexadecimal notations.

```
NUMBER := 115 DIV 10
```

9. Evaluate

a. `-3 ** 2`
b. `0 ** (-2)`
c. `(-1) ** 4`
d. `3 ** (-3)`

10. Rewrite the following construction using the OTHERWISE clause.

```
IF (A <> 1) OR (A <> 2) OR (A <> 3)
    THEN BEGIN
            X := 0;
            Y := 0
        END
    ELSE CASE A OF
            1 :  X := 10;
            2 :  X := 20;
            3 :  X := 30
        END
```

11. Describe what will happen during execution of this program segment.

```
GRADE := 2;
CASE GRADE OF
    3:  WRITELN ('OK');
    4:  WRITELN ('GOOD');
    5:  WRITELN ('EXCELLENT')
END
```

12. Describe what will happen at run time when the following statement is encountered.

```
AGE [25] := 59
```

if AGE is declared as follows:

```
TYPE
    AGE_TYPE = ARRAY [1..20] OF INTEGER;
VAR
    AGE : AGE_TYPE;
```

13. Describe what will happen at run time when the following statement is encountered.

```
FIRSTLETTER := 'M'
```

if FIRSTLETTER is declared as follows:

```
TYPE
    FIRSTLETTER_TYPE = 'A'..'H';
VAR
    FIRSTLETTER : FIRSTLETTER_TYPE;
```

14. The following declarations have appeared in a program:

```
TYPE
    A = VARYING [9] OF CHAR;
    B = ARRAY [1..12] OF A;
VAR
    MONTH : B;
```

and this assignment has been made:

```
MONTH [4] := 'APRIL'
```

How would you access the second character of MONTH [4]?

15. What will happen if, in the situation described in the previous problem, you try to refer to MONTH [4, 7]?

16. In the same situation, append MONTH [4] with blanks until MONTH [4] is 9 characters long. Do not assume that the current length of MONTH [4] is known.

17. In the same situation, restore the string MONTH [4] to its original value. You are allowed to store the original length but not the original string itself.

18. A long string consists of names followed by social security numbers. The names and the social security numbers are separated by one blank character. For example,

John Smith 032-18-7023 Michael O'Brien 341-76-1212 . . .

Find the social security number immediately after the first occurrence of the name Mark Wexler. If this name is not in the string, an appropriate message should be printed.

19. Write statements that will measure the time used by the computer to execute a FOR loop.

20. Is it necessary to use the OPEN procedure before using a file? If not, why is it provided?

21. Explain the difference between these two program segments.

```
a. READ (FILE1, A, B, C, ERROR := CONTINUE);
   IF STATUS (FILE1) <> 0
       THEN WRITELN ('INPUT ERROR')
   READLN (FILE1, ERROR := CONTINUE)
```

and

```
b. READLN (FILE1, A, B, C, ERROR := CONTINUE);
   IF STATUS (FILE1) <> 0
       THEN WRITELN ('INPUT ERROR')
```

22. In Pascal, a string variable can be used with the WRITE statement to output the entire string. However, in order to read a string, each character must be read and assigned to an element of the string, one at a time. What additional capabilities are provided by VAX-11 Pascal?

23. In Pascal, Boolean values can be written but not read. How about VAX-11 Pascal?

24. In Pascal, values of user-defined ordinal types can be neither written, nor read. How about VAX-11 Pascal?

10 TURBO Pascal

TURBO Pascal, produced by Borland International, is one of several implementations developed for use on microcomputers. It runs on the IBM PC and compatibles, and it has attracted many users because of its remarkable efficiency and inexpensiveness.

TURBO Pascal implements almost all the features of standard Pascal. It also implements quite a few extensions of standard Pascal. TURBO Pascal exists in three slightly different versions that run under the operating systems CP/M-80, CP/M-86, and MS-DOS/PS-DOS, but all material in this chapter applies to all three versions.

The main reference used by the author has been the TURBO Pascal Reference Manual, version 2.0, published by Borland International. In comformity with the style of this book, I zero in on various elements of the language itself rather than on the environment in which the language is used.

The following is a summary of the differences between TURBO Pascal and standard Pascal, including many elements that are left undefined in the latter but are defined in the former.

1. TURBO Pascal is case insensitive.

2. In addition to the reserved words used in standard Pascal, the following seven words are reserved in TURBO Pascal:

ABSOLUTE	INLINE	SHR	XOR
EXTERNAL	SHL	STRING	

Their meaning will be explained later.

3. The range of INTEGER numbers is from -32768 to 32767. The range of REAL numbers is from $1E-38$ to $1E38$. Overflow of arithmetic operations is not detected during integer operations but it causes crashes during real operations.

4. In addition to the INTEGER type, the type BYTE is predefined in TURBO Pascal. The BYTE type is a subrange of the INTEGER type. The variables of this type can take integer values from 0 through 255.

5. A real number is stored in six bytes. The exponent occupies the first byte and the mantissa occupies the other five bytes. This yields eleven significant decimal digits. The exponent range is between -38 and 38.

6. The maximum number of elements in a set is 256.

7. Up to 127 characters of an identifier is stored and they may include underscore characters.

8. A label can be either a number or an identifier.

9. Nonnegative integer constants are allowed in either conventional or hexadecimal notation. A hexadecimal constant is preceded by a dollar sign.

10. There are two ways to include control characters in a string:

- using the ordinal value of a control character preceded by a number sign (#);
- using the circumflex followed by a character.

For example, a backspace can be specified as either ^H (or ^h) or #8.

11. The label declaration part, the constant definition part, the type definition part, the variable declaration part, and the procedure and function declaration part may appear in any order, and each of them may appear more than once.

12. The constant PI with ten digits after the decimal point is predefined.

13. Three bitwise operators are defined: integer NOT, shift left (SHL) and shift right (SHR). The first one is a unary operator performing bitwise negation. The shift operators take two operands both of which must be integer.

If

    A := B SHL C

and

    D := E SHR F

then the value of A is the value of B shifted to the left by C bits. The value of D is the value of E shifted to the right by F bits. The integer NOT operator comes before the multiplicative operators in the order of precedence. The shift operators have the same precedence as the multiplicative operators.

14. The exclusive OR operator (XOR) is defined for both integer and Boolean operands. The standard OR operator (inclusive OR) is defined for integer as well as for Boolean operands. The integer versions of both OR operators perform corresponding bitwise functions. The difference between the exclusive and inclusive OR operators is shown in the following truth table for the Boolean versions.

1st operand	2nd operand	OR	XOR
TRUE	TRUE	TRUE	FALSE
TRUE	FALSE	TRUE	TRUE
FALSE	TRUE	TRUE	TRUE
FALSE	FALSE	FALSE	FALSE

Both operators have the same precedence as the additive operators.

15. The CASE statement can include the ELSE clause. If it is included, it specifies the statement to be executed if the value of the CASE expression is not in the constant list. A CASE constant list can include subranges.

16. In standard Pascal, the functions ORD and CHR are inverses of one another only with respect to CHAR data, even though the function ORD is defined for all scalar types. In TURBO Pascal, an ordinal value can be converted to a value of any scalar type. For example, let the type DAY be defined as follows:

```
DAY = (MON, TUE, WED, THU, FRI, SAT, SUN);
```

Then, not only does ORD (FRI) equal 4 (which holds true in standard Pascal) but DAY (4) equals FRI as well (which does not hold true in standard Pascal because DAY is not a function).

17. The option that verifies that all values assigned to variables of subrange types are within the subranges can be specified at compile time.

18. The reserved word STRING is used to define string types as follows:

```
TYPE
    <name> = STRING[<max>];
```

The type <name> is a string containing <max> or fewer characters, where <max> is an integer constant not exceeding 255.

19. The plus operator, +, can be used to concatenate several strings.

20. The relational operators can be used with strings of different lengths. In such cases as

$$\text{'MARK' and 'MARKET'}$$

the longer string is considered the greater; however, it was noticed by B. Webster and D. Wendt in "A Review of TURBO Pascal," Softalk IBM, March 1984, that this part of TURBO Pascal contained a bug. Namely, both

$$\text{'MARK' < 'MARKET'}$$

and

$$\text{'MARKET' < 'MARK'}$$

returned FALSE. It was also reported in the same article that Borland International was working on fixing the bug.

21. A number of string procedures and functions are available:

- The procedure DELETE deletes a substring of a given string.
- The procedure INSERT inserts one string into another.
- The procedure STR converts an integer or real number into a string consisting of its digits, and if appropriate, a decimal point and the letter E.
- The procedure VAL performs the opposite function: it converts a string of digits and possibly a decimal point and the letter E into an integer or real value represented by that string.
- The function COPY returns a substring of a given string.
- The function CONCAT concatenates two or more strings.
- The function LENGTH returns the number of characters in a string.
- The function POS searches for the first occurrence of a pattern within a string. The function returns an integer value indicating the position of the first character of the pattern in the string or 0 if the pattern is not found.

22. Constants can be defined together with their types, and there are different rules for the use of typed constants. Constants of structured types are allowed.

23. There are several additional file handling procedures and functions:

- The procedure ASSIGN creates an association between a disk file and a file variable.
- The procedure SEEK allows the programmer to move the file window to a component specified by its position.
- The procedure ERASE deletes a disk file.
- The function FILEPOS returns the current position of the file window.
- The function FILESIZE returns the number of components in a file.

24. GET and PUT are not implemented but READ and WRITE can be used for all types of files rather than just for text files.

25. Many other standard procedures and functions are available including

- Several screen control procedures.
- The function FRAC, which returns the fractional portion of a real number.
- The function RANDOM, which returns pseudorandom numbers uniformly distributed between 0 and 1.

26. The compiler can be forced to store a variable at a specific memory address.

27. The standard function ADDR returns the memory address of a given variable, procedure, or a function.

28. The predeclared arrays MEM and MEMW (the latter for the MS-DOS/PS-DOS and CP/M-86 versions only) allow the programmer to access memory directly. The components of the former array are bytes and the components of the latter are words. The subscript specifies the memory address.

29. Machine code operations can be included in a program using the INLINE statement.

30. The procedure PAGE is not implemented in TURBO Pascal.

31. Functions and procedures cannot be passed to other functions or procedures as parameters.

PROBLEMS

1. Which of the following identifiers are valid in TURBO Pascal?

   a. `TESTSCORES`
   b. `testscores`
   c. `TestScores`
   d. `Test_Scores`
   e. `10_Test_Scores`
   f. `This_Is_A_Very_Long_Identifier_But_Is_It_Too_Long`
   g. `Absolute`
   h. `EOF`

2. Are the following two identifiers identical or distinct within a TURBO Pascal program?

   a. `State_income_tax`
   b. `STATE_INCOME_TAX`

3. Are the following pair of identifiers identical or distinct within a TURBO Pascal program?

   a. `The_number_of_people_who_were_born_in_the_world_in_1942`
   b. `The_number_of_people_who_were_born_in_the_world_in_1943`

4. The following line:

   ```
   WHILE{COMMENT 1}I{COMMENT 2}DO
   ```

   a. is the same as a line consisting of the identifier WHILEIDO with two comments inserted into it and, therefore, invalid;
   b. is the same as a line consisting of the identifier WHILEIDO with two comments inserted into it and, therefore, valid;
   c. is the same as a line consisting of the three language elements: WHILE, I and DO properly separated by delimiters (comments). It may be part of a WHILE loop.

   Choose the right answer.

5. Will the following two program segments yield the same result in TURBO Pascal?

   a.
   ```
   NUMBER := 1;
   FOR COUNTER := 1 TO 20
   DO NUMBER := 2 * NUMBER;
   FOR COUNTER := 20 DOWNTO 11
   DO NUMBER := NUMBER DIV 2;
   WRITELN (NUMBER)
   ```

   b.
   ```
   NUMBER := 1;
   FOR COUNTER := 1 TO 10
   DO NUMBER := 2 * NUMBER;
   WRITELN (NUMBER)
   ```

6. Rewrite the following statements using hexadecimal notation.

   a. `A := 100`
   b. `A := 455`
   c. `A := 13`

7. Rewrite the following statements using decimal notation.

   a. `A := $302`
   b. `A := $FA`
   c. `A := $B2E`

8. What WRITE statement will cause the word HELLO to be printed and underlined?

9. Is **– A * B** evaluated as **(– A) * B** or as **– (A * B)** ?

10. Evaluate NOT $8016.

11. Evaluate 11 OR 14.

12. Evaluate 11 XOR 14.

13. Evaluate **(2 = 4) OR ('A' < 'B') XOR ('2' <> '3')** .

14. Rewrite the following construction using the ELSE clause:

```
IF (A <> 1) OR (A <> 2) OR (A <> 3)
    THEN BEGIN
             X := 0;
             Y := 0
         END
    ELSE CASE A OF
             1 : X := 10;
             2 : X := 20;
             3 : X := 30
         END
```

15. Simplify this construction using subranges:

```
CASE SCORE OF
    1, 2, 3, 4 : WRITELN ('YOU FLUNKED');
    5, 6, 7    : WRITELN ('YOU PASSED BUT IMPROVEMENT
                           IS NEEDED');
    8, 9, 10   : WRITELN ('YOU PASSED')
END
```

16. Evaluate the following expressions:

a. `'1967' > 'MARK'`
b. `'MARK' <= 'Mark'`
c. `'MARK' < 'MARKET'`
d. `'M' + 'A' + 'R' + 'K' = 'MA' + 'RK'`

17. The type of the variable NAME is defined as follows:

```
TYPE
    TYPE_OF_NAME = STRING [20]
```

What will happen if too short or too long a string is assigned to NAME, for example,

```
or  NAME := 'OLGA PEKELNY'
    NAME := 'DWIGHT DAVID EISENHOWER'
```

18. NUMBER is an integer variable. Write a program segment that will print the value of NUMBER so that every two consecutive digits are separated by one blank.

19. Find and correct the error in this program segment. (Assume that all necessary declarations have been made).

```
A := '135';
B := '14';
C := A * B
```

20. What is the output of this program segment?

```
NAME := 'TENNESSEE WILLIAMS';
FIRST_NAME := 'ALFRED';

DELETE (NAME, 7, 12);
INSERT (FIRST_NAME + ' ', NAME, 0);
NAME [12] := 'Y';
NAME := NAME + 'ON';
WRITELN (NAME)
```

21. What is the output of this program segment?

```
A := 'TURBO PASCAL';
WRITELN (POS ('PAC', A))
```

22. Is this constant definition legal?

```
TYPE
   X = ARRAY [1..4] OF INTEGER;
CONST
   A : X = (10, 103, -2, 0)
```

23. A long string consists of names followed by dates of birth. The names and the dates of birth are separated by one blank character. For example,

```
JOHN SMITH 02/17/1945 MICHAEL O'BRIEN 06/11/1932 ...
```

Find the date immediately after the name MARK WEXLER. If the name is not found in the string, an appropriate message should be printed.

24. In standard Pascal, a string variable can be used with the WRITE statement to output the entire string. However, in order to read a string, each character must be read and assigned to an element of the string, one at a time. What additional capabilities are provided by TURBO Pascal?

25. In VAX-II Pascal, but not in standard Pascal, user-defined ordinal types can be both written and read. How about TURBO Pascal?

26. INTEGRATE is a procedure with the following heading:

    PROCEDURE INTEGRATE (FUNCTION F (X : REAL) : REAL; ...);

    which computes the integral of F(X). Let us assume that the function LINEAR has been declared and the following procedure call is used:

    INTEGRATE (LINEAR ...)

    Is this valid?

11 Basic Concepts: Solutions

ALGORITHMS AND PROGRAMS

1. Instructions two and three may be contradictory if the exit marked "Main Street" is located not exactly five miles from the entrance. If, on the other hand, the entrance and the exit are exactly five miles apart, then information contained in either one of the instructions two or three is redundant.

2. Here is an algorithm written in pseudocode.

```
MAX = < X >
If < Y > is greater than MAX
       then MAX = < Y >
       else do nothing
If < Z > is greater than MAX
       then MAX = < Z >
       else do nothing.
```

The same algorithm depicted as a flowchart may look as shown in Fig. 11-1.

Try to generalize this algorithm for use when there are more than three numbers.

3. After execution of this algorithm, X will contain the smallest of the three numbers, Y will contain the middle one and Z, the largest one. To see the need for step 3,

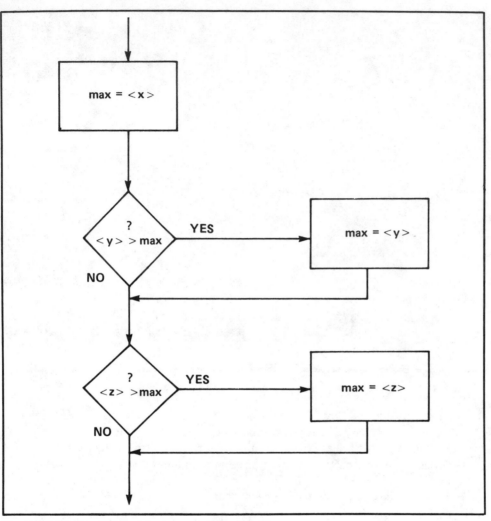

Fig. 11-1. A flowchart of the minimum computation algorithm.

consider the case where the initial contents of X, Y, and Z are 3, 2 and 1, respectively.

4. Here is an algorithm written in pseudocode.

```
COUNTER is 0
If < X > equals < Y >
        then add 1 to COUNTER
        else do nothing
If < Y > equals < Z >
        then add 1 to COUNTER
        else do nothing
```

```
If < X > equals < Z >
        then add 1 to COUNTER
        else do nothing
If COUNTER equals 0
        then print 0
        else print 1.
```

5. Suppose X and Y are memory locations, and $<X>$ and $<Y>$ are their contents. First, why does the following algorithm not accomplish the goal?

```
X   <====   < Y >
Y   <====   < X >.
```

(Here A $<====$ $<B>$ means: the value of $<B>$ is assigned to A.) Simply because after the first step the contents of X would be lost and at the end both X and Y would contain $<Y>$. Let us introduce a temporary memory location Z and denote its contents by $<Z>$. Then the following algorithm is free from the aforementioned flaw.

```
Z   <====   < Y >
Y   <====   < X >
X   <====   < Z >
```

The next algorithm seems artificial but it accomplishes the same goal without using Z.

```
X   <====   < X > + < Y >
Y   <====   < X > - < Y >
X   <====   < X > - < Y >
```

Apply this algorithm to a numerical example.

• Can you modify the algorithm by substituting multiplication and division for addition and subtraction?
• Does your algorithm handle the case where the content of one of the memory locations is 0?

Consider the case where there are several memory locations $X_1, X_2, \ldots, X_N$ and the goal is to change their contents as follows:

$$X_1 <==== <X_2>$$
$$X_2 <==== <X_3>$$

. . . .

$$X_{N-1} <==== <X_N>$$
$$X_N <==== <X_1>$$

6. A

7. B.

8. C.

9. B.

10. a. Compile-time error.
    b. Neither.
    c. Compile-time error.
    d. Compile-time error (unless there is another procedure called RITE).
    e. Compile time error (unless the misspelled name happens to be the name of an-
       other variable).
    f. Run-time error.
    g. Compile-time error.
    h. Neither.
    i. Run-time error.

11. B and C.

MAJOR PARTS OF A PASCAL PROGRAM

1. Only a and f are required.

2.
```
PROGRAM SIMPLE (OUTPUT);
BEGIN
    WRITELN
END.
```

3. No effect whatsoever so long as it is a valid identifier.

4. No, the entire comment may be enclosed between one pair of curly brackets.

5. No. Only {THIS IS AN EXAMPLE OF NESTED COMMENTS {EXAMPLE}
   will be treated as a comment. A comment ends at the first closing curly bracket.
   The compiler will try to interpret the rest of the line as a statement and probably
   crash.

6. All the statements between the two comments will be treated as a continuation
   of the first comment and, therefore, ignored.

7. (* and *).

8. a - legally; b, c and d - illegally.

9. Only e.

10. a. This is not an error. Labels do not have to be consecutive.
    b. This is not an error. Labels do not have to appear in the increasing order. However, a program in which the labels appear in the increasing order is more readable. Incidentally, that is why the use of the labels 100, 200 and 300 is preferable to that of 1, 2 and 3. Should you decide to modify the program and insert one more label, you could do that without breaking the increasing order.
    c. This is a compile-time error: it defects the entire purpose of using labels.

11. Only MAXINT (maximum integer number) is a predefined constant. However, its specific value is implementation dependent. It may be as small as 32767 (or $2^{15} - 1$) on microcomputers and as large as 281474976710655 (or $2^{48} - 1$) on the CDC 6000. All other constants have specific values in every implementation but there are no standard identifiers associated with them. If a programmer needs them, they can be defined explicitly.

12. SALESTAX because it is self-explanatory.

13. Yes, it is a string constant. It cannot be assigned to a character variable.

14. The last definition is invalid: all constants must have values before program execution.

15. They are valid but confusing.

16.
```
PROGRAM CIRCLE (INPUT,OUTPUT);
CONST
    PI = 3.14;
VAR
    RADIUS, CIRCUMFERENCE : REAL;
BEGIN
    WRITELN('PLEASE, ENTER RADIUS');
    READLN(RADIUS);
    AREA := PI * RADIUS * RADIUS;
    CIRCUMFERENCE := 2.0 * PI * RADIUS;
    WRITELN('AREA IS ',AREA,'CIRCUMFERENCE IS ',
    CIRCUMFERENCE

END.
```

This program is more maintainable. Should you decide to use 3.14159 rather than 3.14 for PI, all changes will be confined to one place. Another advantage of using constants is that they make programs self-explanatory, provided that the constant names are descriptive enough.

17. No difference whatsoever.

18. b.

19. It is undefined in standard Pascal.

20. The variable Y was not initialized.

IDENTIFIERS AND ASSIGNMENTS

1. a. Valid.
   b. Valid, but on some installations not all characters will be stored.
   c. Valid. Standard Pascal requires that only uppercase letters be included in the character set. Some installations extend the character set by including lowercase letters as well, but they may or may not distinguish between, say, A and a. In the language of computer science they may be case sensitive or case insensitive. To complicate the issue further, it is possible that while your installation includes lowercase letters, you may be unable to take advantage of that if your terminal only allows you to type only upper case letters.
   d. Invalid: blanks within identifiers are not allowed.
   e. Valid.
   f. Invalid: special characters within identifiers are not allowed.
   g. Invalid: RECORD is a reserved word.
   h. Invalid: see d.
   i. Invalid: the first character must be a letter.
   j. Valid, but see b.
   k. Invalid in standard Pascal because it includes a special character. However, some installations relax this rule by letting the underline character appear within identifiers. Usually, the underline character separates two words, thereby making the identifier more readable.
   l. Invalid because of the special character.
   m. Invalid: see i.
   n. Valid, but see b.
   o. Valid.

2. The answer depends on the implementation. Some installations store only the first 8 characters of an identifier, while others remember considerably more characters. If your implementation remembers fewer than 17 characters, it cannot differentiate between foregoing identifiers and, therefore, they will be treated as identical.

3. No. A character variable can store only one character.

4. No, it is illegal.

5. Yes, it may despite the fact that EXP is the name of a standard function.

6. a. Invalid: the assignment operator is a colon immediately followed by an equals sign.
   b. Invalid: see a.
   c. Valid.
   d. Valid.
   e. Invalid: only a variable may be to the left of the assignment operator.
   f. Valid: Y is divided by the value of the variable ZERO, not by zero.

7. In the first case A, B and C will be 2, 3 and 2, respectively. The results do depend on the sequence in which the statements are executed. In the second case, for example, the results will be 3, 3 and 1.

8. a. In the former case, the value of A becomes equal to the current value of B, where B can be another variable, a constant, or a function. In the latter case, the value of A becomes equal to the character B (it is assumed that A is a character variable).
   b. In the former case, A must be an integer or real variable; whereas in the latter case, it must be a character variable. Incidentally, from this example you can see the problem that would arise if 7 were allowed to be an identifier.

9. Yes, there is. The latter assignment is invalid.

10. Yes, there is. The latter assignment is invalid.

11. Yes, it may, if A is a Boolean variable. Then its value will be TRUE or FALSE depending on whether the current values of B and C are equal or not.

12. No effect whatsoever.

INPUT AND OUTPUT FEATURES.

1.
```
PROGRAM SQUARE(OUTPUT);
BEGIN
     WRITELN('--------');
     WRITELN('!        !');
     WRITELN('!        !');
     WRITELN('!        !');
     WRITELN('!        !');
     WRITELN('!        !');
     WRITELN('!        !');
     WRITELN('--------')
END.
```

2.
```
PROGRAM NAME(OUTPUT);
BEGIN
```

```
WRITELN('******   *      *    *****  ******  *      *  ******');
WRITELN('*        *      *  *          *     **     *  *');
WRITELN('*        *      *  *          *     * *    *  *');
WRITELN('*****    *      *  *****    *****    *  *   *  *****');
WRITELN('*        *      *  *   *    *        *   *  *  *');
WRITELN('*          *  *    *    *    *        *    **  *');
WRITELN('******      ***     ****   ******  *      *  ******')
END.
```

3.  ```
    PROGRAM BACKWARD(INPUT,OUTPUT);
    VAR
        C1, C2, C3 : CHAR;
    BEGIN
        WRITELN('PLEASE, TYPE THREE LETTER WORD');
        READLN(C1,C2,C3);
        WRITELN(C3,C2,C1)
    END;
    ```

4. One single quote.

5. Three asterisks will be printed horizontally, in the former case, and vertically, in the latter case.

6. Three lines of input data will be discarded.

7. Yes. In both cases 5 will be assigned to X but in the former case a blank will be assigned to Y whereas in the latter case a C will be assigned to Y.

8. a. 41 is assigned to A, 7 is assigned to B, -3.7 is assigned to C or in short: $A <=== 41, B <=== 7, C <=== -3.7$.
   b. $A <=== 41, B === 7, C <=== -3.7$ (the number of blanks between values is irrelevant).
   c. $A <=== 41, B <=== 7, C <=== -3.7$ (carriage returns separating two values are ignored).
   d. $A <=== 41, B <=== 7, C <=== -3.7$ (extra characters of the line are discarded).
   e. The program will wait forever for the user to enter the last value (if it is an interactive program).
   f. $A <=== 417$, then a run-time error, since the program encounters a real value where it expects to find an integer value.
   g. A run-time error for the same reason as in f.
   h. A run-time error, since the program encounters an unexpected character where it expects to find a digit.

9. a. A compile-time error: A B is an invalid identifier.
    ```

b. The compiler will try to interpret AB as an identifier. If AB has not been declared, the compiler will detect an error. Otherwise it will try to assign the value intended for A to AB.

c. The value intended for A will be assigned to B and vice versa. If A and B happen to have different types, this will cause a run-time error.

10.
```
WRITELN ('          X        ¦    Y    ¦   Z     ');
WRITELN ('                   ¦         ¦         ');
WRITELN ('------------------------------------');
WRITELN ('                   ¦         ¦         ');
WRITELN (X,'  ¦  ',Y,'  ¦    ',Z)
```

The last statement is based on a certain assumption about the default field width which is implementation dependent.

11. Assume that the default field width for integers is 10 columns. Then

a.   17   5   1967
b. X =   17Y =   5Z =   1967
c. X =17 Y =5 Z =1967
d. X = 17,   Y = 5,   Z = 1967

12. a.
```
WRITELN (X);
WRITELN (Y);
WRITELN (Z)
```

b.
```
WRITELN (X:1);
WRITELN (Y:1);
WRITELN (Z:1)
```

13. The same effect will be achieved by this statement:

```
WRITE (' ' : 10)
```

(One blank between the single quotes).

14. a. 123.48   d. 123.5
    b. 123.48   e. 123.4800
    c. 123.48

15. It is a valid statement. Field widths may be constants or expressions. In the foregoing example, the output will be   3.1.

16. The use of the standard procedure PAGE. It is more convenient because you do

not have to count the number of lines to skip over. Besides, the use of PAGE makes the program more robust. Should you later decide to change the table length from 10 to 11, you will not have to readjust spacing.

17. Since the number of single quotes must always be even, the compiler will detect the error.

12 Expressions: Solutions

1. a. valid
   b. valid
   c. invalid: decimal points are not allowed
   d. invalid: commas are not allowed
   e. invalid: a blank within a number is not allowed
   f. valid
   g. invalid: decimal points are not allowed
   h. valid
   i. valid

2. a. valid
   b. valid
   c. invalid: there must be at least one digit to the right of the decimal point
   d. invalid: there must be at least one digit to the left of the decimal point
   e. invalid: there is no decimal point
   f. valid
   g. invalid: a comma is not allowed
   h. invalid: there must be at least one digit to the left of the decimal point
   i. valid

3. a. b. c. and d. valid

e. invalid: the exponent must be an integer
f. g. h. i. and j. valid

4. a. 5.0E3   c. 6.3E – 6
   b. – 4.375E3   d. – 1.1E1

5. a. 4700.0   c. – 4700.00
   b. 0.0047   d. – 0.0047

6. a. valid
   b. valid
   c. valid
   d. invalid: both operands must be integer
   e. valid
   f. invalid: since 3.0 * 14 is evaluated first, a real operand will be used with DIV which is not allowed
   g. invalid: the exponent is an expression
   h. invalid: the mantissa is an expression

7. a. valid
   b. invalid: a real value may not be assigned to an integer variable
   c. valid
   d. invalid: a real value may not be assigned to an integer variable
   e. valid
   f. valid
   g. valid
   h. invalid: since CI / DI is evaluated first, a real operand will be used with DIV, which is not allowed
   i. valid
   j. invalid: a real value may not be assigned to an integer variable

8. a. valid only if B is a character variable
   b. invalid: an integer value may not be assigned to a character variable
   c. valid
   d. invalid
   e. invalid: a character variable can take on single character values only
   f. valid
   g. invalid: the operator – is not defined with character operands
   h. invalid: – 7 is not a single character value
   i. invalid: the operator – is not defined with character operands
   j. invalid: the addition of character values is not defined

ARITHMETIC AND BOOLEAN OPERATORS
1. a. 18
   b. 0
   c. 4.0

2. a. `17 - ((4 * 3) DIV 7)`
   b. `(4.6 * 3) - (8 / 2)`
   c. `((A DIV A) DIV A) * B`

3. a. `A - 3.4 - (7 * NUMBER + 4)`
   b. `-(B - C) * 6.0`

4. The operator MOD has a higher precedence than the unary operator $-$. Therefore, $-$ A MOD B is evaluated as $-$ (A MOD B).

5. Let us apply the following identity:

   `A MOD B = A - ((A DIV B) * B)`

   a. 1   c. -1
   b. undefined d. -1

   Note that the result does not depend on whether -5 MOD 2 is interpreted as $-$ (5 MOD 2) or as (-5) MOD 2.

6. It is sufficient to remember that the quotient is always rounded toward zero.

   a. -2 c. 2
   b. -2 d. 0

   Note that the result does not depend on whether -5 DIV 2 is interpreted as $-$ (5 DIV 2) or as (-5) DIV 2.

7. The result is undefined in standard Pascal. Depending on the implementation, the program may crash or produce an unexpected value.

8. `NUMBER := 7 * (4 - 2 * NUMBER)`

9. Pascal has no operator for exponentiation. Exponentiation can be accomplished using the standard functions EXP and LN.

10. a. `MINUTE DIV 60`
    b. `MINUTE DIV (60 * 24)`
    c. `MINUTE DIV (60 * 24 * 7)`

11. a.
```
MYSTERY MOD 10      DIV 1     * 10000 +
MYSTERY MOD 100     DIV 10    * 1000  +
MYSTERY MOD 1000    DIV 100   * 100   +
MYSTERY MOD 10000   DIV 1000  * 10    +
MYSTERY MOD 100000  DIV 10000 * 1
```

b.
```
MYSTERY MOD 10     DIV 1    *  100   +
MYSTERY MOD 100    DIV 10   *  1000  +
MYSTERY MOD 1000   DIV 100  *  10000 +
MYSTERY MOD 10000  DIV 1000 *  1     +
MYSTERY MOD 100000 DIV 10000 * 10
```

12. a. Invalid. Relational operators have a lower precedence than arithmetic operators and, therefore, our expression is equivalent to 3 > (4 AND 7) = 5. But (4 AND 7) is already invalid.

   b. Invalid. The expression is equivalent to (4 < 5) < 6 or TRUE < 6, which is valid.

   c. Invalid. < = is one symbol and blanks between < and = are not allowed.

   d. Valid.

   e. Valid.

   f. Valid.

   g. Invalid. Since NOT has the highest precedence, it may not be followed by OR.

   h. Valid.

   i. Valid.

13. a. FALSE
    b. TRUE
    c. FALSE
    d. TRUE

14. a. **(A OR B) OR ((NOT C) AND D)**.
    b. **((NOT A) AND (7 <> Y)) OR (X = Y)**

15. a. **NOT A AND NOT B OR C**
    b. **(NOT A OR NOT B) AND C**

16. Valid. FALSE will be printed.

17. No, Boolean variables cannot be arguments of READ or READLN statements.

18. It may be invalid.

19. a. TRUE (because 'L' < > 'W')
    b. FALSE (because 'OLGA' is lexically greater than 'MARK').
    c. FALSE (because 'MARY' is lexically greater than 'MARK').
    d. Invalid (because relational operators may be used to make comparisons only between pairs of strings of the same length.

STANDARD FUNCTIONS

1. a. 4, b. 16.0, c. 5.0, d. 1.0, e. 0.0, f. the argument of the Pascal standard trigonometric functions is always given in radians, rather than degrees. The result can be computed using a pocket calculator. Namely, g. 0.0, h. 1.0, i. even though

the values of ORD ('B') and ORD ('D') depend on the implementation, all capital Latin letters are always ordered alphabetically. Hence, ORD ('D') – ORD ('B') is 2. j. the result depends on the implementation. k. 'M', 1. TRUE, m. 2, n. 2.0, o. −9, p. −10, q. approximately 0.7854, r. 'B'.

2. a. `(X + Y + Z)/(SQRT (SQR (X)+ SQR (Y)+ SQR (Z)))`
   b. `SQR (A * B * C)`
   c. `LN (1.0 + ABS ((A + B) / (A - B)))`
   d. `2.0 * SIN ((X + Y) / 2.0) * COS ((X - Y) / 2.0)`

3. a. 0.662, b. 54.6, c. 1.37.

4. No, here is a counterexample: TRUNC (2.9 + 3.9) equals 6 whereas TRUNC (2.9) + TRUNC (3.9) equals 5.

5. No, here is a counterexample: ROUND (2.3 + 3.4) equals 6 whereas ROUND (2.3) + ROUND (3.4) equals 5.

6. ORD ('A') is the ordinal number of the character Λ. ORD (Λ) is the ordinal number of the value of A. In the latter case A may be a variable, constant, or a function.

7. COS is not a reserved word in Pascal. A programmer is free to introduce such a function, in which case COS (1.0) will be 0.5. However, then it will be impossible to use the function COS in its regular definition.

8. `NOT ODD (NUMBER)`

9. No, TRUNC (3.7) is the integer value 3.

10. a. 65, b. 61, c. 6, d. j (lower case j).

11. Yes, they are equal to 19 and −71.

12. The value is undefined in standard Pascal.

13. a. `ROUND (X * 100.0) / 100.0`
    b. `TRUNC (X * 100.0) / 100.0`

14. a. `ROUND (X / 100.0) * 100.0`
    b. `TRUNC (X / 100.0) * 100.0`

15. Yes.

16. The expression yields 0.0 when X is negative, and X otherwise.

17. Even though the expression X * SQR (X) will do the job in part a, we will use a

general approach based on this identity: $x^Y = e^{y \ln x}$

Hence, a. **EXP (3.0 * LN (X))**
    b. **EXP (LN (X) / 5.0)**
    c. **EXP (1.35 * LN (X))**

The solution to d is based on the algebraic formula $\quad \log_a b \quad \dfrac{\log_c b}{\log_c a}$

Hence, d. **LN (X) / LN (2.0)**

18. The answers are based on known trigonometric relationships, such as the following:

$\sin^2 x + \cos^2 x = 1$

$\tan x = \dfrac{\sin x}{\cos x}$

$\csc x = \dfrac{1}{\sin x}$

$\arcsin x + \arccos x = \dfrac{\pi}{2}$

$\cot x = \dfrac{\cos x}{\sin x}$

$\sec x = \dfrac{1}{\cos x}$

$\arctan x + \mathrm{arccot}\, x = \dfrac{\pi}{2}$

a. **SIN (X) / COS (X)**
b. **COS (X) / SIN (X)**
c. **1.0 / COS (X)**
d. **1.0 / SIN (X)**
e. **ARCTAN (X / SQRT (1.0 - SQR (X)))**
f. **ARCTAN (SQRT (1.0 - SQR (X)) / X)**
g. **approximately 1.57 - ARCTAN (X)**
h. **ARCTAN (SQRT (1.0 - SQR (1.0 / X)) * X)**
i. **ARCTAN (1.0 / X * SQRT (1.0 - SQR (1.0 / X)))**

13 Control Statements: Solutions

THE IF STATEMENT

1. ```
10 IS EVEN
AND DON'T FORGET THAT ODD RETURNS BOOLEAN VALUES
```

2. The Boolean values are ordered in such a way that FALSE < TRUE. Therefore, the following message will be printed:

```
TRUE IS GREATER THAN FALSE
```

3. ```
IF A < B
    THEN BEGIN
            X := 1;
            READ (Y)
        END
    ELSE BEGIN
            X := 2;
            READ (Z)
        END
```

4. ```
IF (A <> B) OR (MYINCOME >= YOURINCOME)
    THEN I := J
    ELSE I := -J
```
```

```
5. IF (RATE > 0) AND (RATE < 1)
        THEN A := 0
        ELSE A := 1
```

6. In construction A, U becomes equal to W if and only if A > = B. In construction
   B, U becomes equal to W if and only if the following two conditions are satisfied:

   1. **A < B**
   2. **C <> D**

   If the statement brackets BEGIN and END are omitted, then the construction A
   will be interpreted as construction B.

7.
```
PROGRAM LINEAR (INPUT, OUTPUT);
    {SOLVES LINEAR EQUATIONS OF TYPE A * X + B = 0}
VAR
    A, B, X : REAL;
BEGIN
    WRITELN ('PLEASE, ENTER A AND B');
    READLN (A, B);
    IF (A <> 0)
        THEN BEGIN
                X := -B / A;
                WRITELN ('X IS ',X)
             END
        ELSE
            WRITELN ('A MUST NOT BE ZERO')
END.
```

8. Let us outline a program solving equations of type

   A * SQR (X) + B * X + C = 0.

   First, consider two cases: A = 0 and A<> 0. In the former case, the equation
   is a linear equation. In the latter case, consider three subcases:

   1. **SQR (B) − 4 * A * C > 0**
   2. **SQR (B) − 4 * A * C = 0**
   3. **SQR (B) − 4 * A * C < 0**

   In case 3, for example, the following segment will do the job (notations are self-
   explanatory):

```
IMAGINARYPART := (SQR (B) - 4 * A * C) / (2 * A);
REALPART := -B / (2 * A);
WRITELN ('ROOT 1 IS ',REALPART,'+',IMAGINARYPART,' * I');
WRITELN ('ROOT 2 IS ',REALPART,'-',IMAGINARYPART,' * I')
```

138

```
9. a.  WRITELN ('PLEASE, ENTER NUMBER BETWEEN O AND 100');
       READLN (NUMBER);
       IF (NUMBER < 0) OR (NUMBER > 100)
           THEN WRITELN ('NUMBER IS OUTSIDE THE GIVEN RANGE');
       <next segment>

   b.  WRITELN ('PLEASE, ENTER NUMBER BETWEEN O AND 100');
       READLN (NUMBER);
       IF (NUMBER >= 0) AND (NUMBER <= 100)
           THEN
                 <next segment>
           ELSE WRITELN ('NUMBER IS OUTSIDE THE GIVEN RANGE')
       END.

   c.  (with option A after the second failure).
       WRITELN ('PLEASE, ENTER NUMBER BETWEEN O AND 100);
       READLN (NUMBER);
       IF (NUMBER < 0) OR (NUMBER > 100)
           THEN
                 BEGIN
                     WRITELN ('NUMBER IS INVALID, TRY AGAIN');
                     READLN (NUMBER);
                     IF (NUMBER < 0) OR (NUMBER > 100)
                         THEN WRITELN ('NUMBER IS INVALID AGAIN')
                 END;
   d.  <next segment>

       (with option A if all attempts fail).
       COUNTER := 1;
       REPEAT
           WRITELN ('PLEASE, ENTER NUMBER BETWEEN O AND 100');
           READLN (NUMBER);
           COUNTER := COUNTER + 1
       UNTIL (COUNTER > 3) OR (NUMBER >= 0) AND (NUMBER <= 100);
       <next segment>

   e.  REPEAT
           WRITELN ('PLEASE, ENTER NUMBER BETWEEN O AND 100');
           READLN (NUMBER)
       UNTIL (NUMBER >= 0) AND (NUMBER <= 100)
```

10. The value of A will be 1. The semicolon after THEN signifies the end of the IF statement. In other words, empty statements are executed whether or not A >= 7, and the next compound statement is executed in either case.

THE CASE STATEMENT

1. 2.

2. **SUM = 4.**

3. The constant list contains the constant 4 twice.

4. The case expression may equal 10, but 10 is not on the constant list.

5. One of the constants is real.

6. X and Y are not constants.

7. The case expression and the constants are of different types.

8. The case expression includes a real number.

9. There is no semicolon after the first statement.

10. No.

11. 0 and 1. Proof: any integer N can be represented as either 3K or 3K + 1 or 3K + 2, where K is an integer,
    but **SQR (3K) MOD 3 = 0, SQR (3K + 1) MOD 3 = 1, SQR (3K + 2) MOD 3 = 1.**

12.
```
PROGRAM MONTHS (INPUT, OUTPUT);
(*THIS PROGRAM PRINTS OUT THE MONTHS OF THE YEAR*)
VAR
    MONTH             : INTEGER;
     EXITCONDITION : CHAR;
BEGIN
    EXITCONDITION := 'N';
    REPEAT
        WRITELN ('ENTER NUMBER FROM 1 TO 12');
        READLN (MONTH);
        IF (MONTH >= 1) AND (MONTH <= 12) THEN
            BEGIN
                CASE MONTH OF
                    1  : WRITELN ('JANUARY');
                    2  : WRITELN ('FEBRUARY');
                    3  : WRITELN ('MARCH');
                    4  : WRITELN ('APRIL');
                    5  : WRITELN ('MAY');
```

```
                        6  : WRITELN ('JUNE');
                        7  : WRITELN ('JULY');
                        8  : WRITELN ('AUGUST');
                        9  : WRITELN ('SEPTEMBER');
                       10  : WRITELN ('OCTOBER');
                       11  : WRITELN ('NOVEMBER');
                       12  : WRITELN ('DECEMBER')
                  END;
                  WRITELN ('IF YOU WANT TO TERMINATE, SAY YES');
                  WRITELN ('OTHERWISE SAY NO');
                  READLN (EXITCONDITION)
            END
        ELSE
           BEGIN
               WRITELN ('THE NUMBER IS NOT BETWEEN 1 AND 12');
               WRITELN ('IF YOU WANT TO TERMINATE, SAY YES');
               WRITELN ('IF YOU WANT TO CONTINUE, SAY NO');
                     READLN (EXITCONDITION)
               END;
         UNTIL EXITCONDITION = 'Y'
      END.


13. IF (K > 0) AND (K <= 10) THEN
       CASE K OF
          8, 9, 10 : X := 1;
             6, 7 : X := 0;
          3, 4, 5 : X := 3;
             1, 2 : X := 4
       END;


14. WRITELN ('ENTER P, U OR R FOR PREMIUM, UNLEADED OR
             REGULAR GASOLINE');
   READLN (GRADE);
   CASE GRADE OF
      'P': PRICE := 1.50;
      'U': PRICE := 1.35;
      'R': PRICE := 1.18
   END;
   WRITELN ('ENTER F, M OR S FOR FULL, MINI- OR SELF-SERVICE');
   READLN (SERVICE);
   WRITELN ('ENTER THE AMOUNT IN GALLONS');
   READLN (AMOUNT);
   CASE SERVICE OF
      'F': COST := AMOUNT * PRICE;
      'M': COST := AMOUNT * PRICE * 0.95;
```

```
      'S': COST := AMOUNT * PRICE * 0.90
END
```

15. If the user enters a series of numbers (scores) between 0 and 10, the program breaks
    them down into five categories according to the following table.

Categories	Numbers Entered
1	0, 1, 2, 3
2	4
3	5, 6
4	7, 8
5	9, 10

The program computes and prints the total number of entries in each category.
These numbers are denoted F, D, C, B and A for categories 1, 2, 3, 4 and 5, respectively. The user can terminate the program by entering any number less than 0.

16. Let us assume that both TRANSACTION and COMMISSION are integer variables.
    In the following program segment all amounts are rounded down to the nearest
    integer.

```
IF (TRANSACTION >= 0) AND (TRANSACTION <= 10000) THEN
    BEGIN
        CASE (TRANSACTION DIV 1000) OF
                0, 1, 2 : COMMISSION := 18 + TRANSACTION *
                    12 DIV 1000;
                    3, 4, 5 : COMMISSION := 36 + TRANSACTION *
                    6 DIV 1000;
            6, 7, 8, 9, 10 : COMMISSION := 57 + TRANSACTION *
                    3 DIV 1000
        END;
        WRITELN (' COMMISSION = ', COMMISSION);
    END
ELSE
    WRITELN ('TRANSACTION IS NOT WITHIN THE GIVEN RANGE');
```

17.
```
WRITELN ('ENTER TWO OPERANDS');
READLN (OP1,OP2);
WRITELN ('ENTER OPERATOR');
READLN (OPERATOR)
IF (OPERATOR IN ['+', '-', '*', '/'])
    THEN
            CASE OPERATOR OF
```

```
           '+':       WRITELN (OP1 + OP2);
           '-':       WRITELN (OP1 - OP2);
           '*':       WRITELN (OP1 * OP2);
           '/':       WRITELN (OP1 / OP2)
        END
     ELSE WRITELN ('INVALID OPERATOR')
```

18. Here is an outline of the program. Let us assume that the students were born between 1900 and 1985. Note that December 31, 1985, is a Tuesday. First, we compute the total number of days between the birthday and December 31, 1985. Let the integer variables DAY, MONTH, and YEAR be the day, month, and year of the birth, respectively. Then, the expression for the total number of days will almost be

$$(1985 - YEAR) * 365 + (12 - MONTH) * 30 + (31 - DAY)$$

The only complication arises from the facts that some months have 28 or 31 days and some years have 366 days. The number of leap years can be obtained using standard integer operators while the first correction is best handled by a CASE statement.

Finally, if the modulus of the total number of days with respect to 7 is 0, then the birth occurred on Tuesday, if it is 1, then the birth occurred on Monday, etc. A simple CASE statement will conclude the program.

LOOPS

1. We will not assume that the reader is familiar with arithmetic progressions. The following solutions utilize straightforward summation.

    a.
```
SUM := 0;
FOR NUMBER := 1 TO 100
DO SUM := SUM + NUMBER
```

    b.
```
SUM := 0;
FOR NUMBER := 1 TO 50
DO SUM := SUM + 2 * NUMBER
```

    c.
```
SUM := 0;
FOR NUMBER := 1 TO 50
DO SUM := SUM + (2 * NUMBER - 1)
```

2. a. Here is a straightforward solution:

```
SUM := 0;
FOR NUMBER := 1 TO 100
DO IF (NUMBER MOD 3 = 0) AND (NUMBER MOD 4 = 0)
        THEN SUM := SUM + NUMBER
```

However, since the set of all numbers divisible by 3 and 4 is the same as the set of all numbers divisible by 12, another solution can be proposed.

```
SUM := 0;
NUMBER := 12;
REPEAT
    SUM := SUM + NUMBER;
    NUMBER := NUMBER + 12
UNTIL NUMBER > 100
```

It is easy to notice that the latter solution requires significantly fewer computer instructions.

```
b.SUM := 0;
  FOR NUMBER 1 to 100
  DO IF (NUMBER MOD 3 <> 0) AND (NUMBER MOD 4 <> 4)
         THEN SUM := SUM + NUMBER
```

3. Let $x_1, x_2, ..., x_N$ be given numbers. Then, their standard deviation may be computed as follows

$$\sqrt{\frac{1}{N} \sum_{i=1}^{N} X_i^2 - \left(\frac{\sum_{i=1}^{N} X_i}{N}\right)^2}$$

This formula is especially convenient for iterative computations in which individual x_i cannot be stored.

```
PROGRAM SUM (INPUT, OUTPUT);
CONST
    SENTINEL = -100;
VAR
    COUNTER : INTEGER;
    NUMBER, SUM, SUMOFSQUARES : REAL;
BEGIN
    COUNTER := 0;
    SUM := 0.0;
    SUMOFSQUARES := 0.0;
    WRITELN ('PLEASE, ENTER A NUMBER');
    READLN (NUMBER);
    WHILE NUMBER <> SENTINEL
    DO BEGIN
```

```
            COUNTER := COUNTER + 1;
            SUM := SUM + NUMBER;
            SUMOFSQUARES := SUMOFSQUARES + SQR (NUMBER)
        END;
    IF COUNTER > 0
        THEN BEGIN
                WRITELN ('MEAN IS ',SUM / COUNTER);
                WRITELN ('STANDARD DEVIATION IS ',
                    SQRT (SUMOFSQUARES / COUNTER - SQR (SUM
                        / COUNTER )))
            END
    END.
```

4. Here is a straightforward solution based on checking out every number.

```
PROGRAM TENNUMBERS (OUTPUT);
VAR
    COUNTER, NUMBER : INTEGER;
BEGIN
    COUNTER := 0;
    NUMBER := 0;
    REPEAT
      NUMBER := NUMBER + 1;
      IF(NUMBER MOD 2 = 1) AND (NUMBER MOD 3 = 1) AND (NUMBER
                                            MOD 5 = 1)
        THEN BEGIN
                WRITELN (NUMBER);
                    COUNTER := COUNTER + 1
                END
        UNTIL COUNTER = 10
    END.
```

A more efficient solution is based on the observation that the numbers with the given property form an arithmetic progression. The first number of the progression is 1 and the common difference is 30 or 2 * 3 * 5. An implementation of this idea is left to the reader.

5. We will use the following fact. A number is prime if and only if it is not divisible by any integers between 1 and SQRT (N).

```
PROGRAM PRIME (INPUT, OUTPUT);
VAR
    FLAG : BOOLEAN;
    NUMBER, COUNTER : INTEGER;
```

```
BEGIN
    FLAG := FALSE;
    WRITELN ('PLEASE, ENTER ANY INTEGER GREATER THAN 2');
    READLN (NUMBER);
    FOR COUNTER := 2 TO ROUND (SQRT (NUMBER))
    DO   IF (NUMBER MOD COUNTER  = 0)
            THEN FLAG := TRUE;
    IF FLAG = FALSE
         THEN WRITELN ('THE NUMBER IS PRIME')
         ELSE WRITELN ('THE NUMBER IS COMPOSITE')
END.
```

6.
```
PROGRAM SIGN (INPUT, OUTPUT);
  CONST
     SENTINEL = -100;
  VAR
     NUMBER, POSITIVE, NEGATIVE : INTEGER;
  BEGIN
     POSITIVE := 0;
     NEGATIVE := 0;
     WRITELN ('PLEASE, ENTER AN INTEGER NUMBER');
     READLN (NUMBER)
     WHILE NUMBER <> -100
     DO BEGIN
            IF NUMBER >= 0
                THEN POSITIVE := POSITIVE + 1
                ELSE NEGATIVE := NEGATIVE + 1;
            WRITELN ('PLEASE, ENTER ANOTHER NUMBER');
            READLN (NUMBER)
        END;
     WRITELN (POSITIVE,' POSITIVE NUMBERS, ',NEGATIVE,'
             NEGATIVE ONES')
  END.
```

7.
```
SUM := 0;
FOR I := 1 TO 10
DO FOR J := 1 TO 10
   DO SUM := SUM + I * J
```

8. Segment A or segment B can be used depending on whether the diagonal elements
   themselves are to be included or excluded.

   a.
```
SUM := 0;
FOR I := 1 TO 10
DO FOR J := I TO 10
```

146

```
          DO SUM := SUM + I * J

    B. SUM := 0;
       FOR I := 1 TO 10
       DO FOR J := I + 1 TO 10
          DO SUM := SUM + I * J
```

```
9. INTEGRAL := 0.0;
   FOR COUNTER := 1 TO TRUNC ((B - A) / H)
   DO INTEGRAL := INTEGRAL + H * EXP(-SQR(A + H * (COUNTER -
                                         1) + H / 2))
```

10. a. The line HELLO will be printed 5 times.
     b. The line HELLO will be printed an infinite number of times or until aborted by
        the operating system.
     c. Same as in B (the counter will never become 5).
     d. Same as in B (the counter will jump over 5).

11. The counter variable was not declared.

12. The counter variable must not be altered within a FOR loop.

13. The final value must not be altered within a FOR loop.

14. The final value must not be a real expression.

15. The types of the counter variable and the initial and final values must be the same.

16. The counter variable must not be an expression.

17.
```
PROGRAM FOUNDIT (INPUT, OUTPUT);
VAR
    GUESS, LETTER : CHAR;
    COUNTER : INTEGER;
BEGIN
    FOR COUNTER := 1 TO 6
    DO BEGIN
            CASE COUNTER OF
                1: LETTER := 'E';
                2: LETTER := 'U';
                3: LETTER := 'R';
                4: LETTER := 'E';
                5: LETTER := 'K';
                6: LETTER := 'A'
        END;
```

```
        REPEAT
                WRITELN ('PLEASE, ENTER YOUR GUESS');
                READLN (GUESS);
                UNTIL LETTER = GUESS
            END;
        WRITELN ('YOU''VE FOUND IT')
    END.
```

18. The same effect can be achieved by introducing an auxiliary variable. Let us write a program segment that will print out every third integer number between 1 and 100 beginning with 3.

```
STEP := 3;
FOR COUNTER := 1 TO 100 DIV STEP
DO BEGIN
    {COUNTER1 IS AN AUXILIARY VARIABLE}
        COUNTER1 := COUNTER * STEP;
        WRITELN (COUNTER1)
    END
```

19. Because of the semicolon after DO, the loop executes an empty statement 10 times. The WRITELN statement is outside the loop body and, therefore, its argument I is undefined.

20. Real numbers can take on values only to a certain accuracy. In effect, there are a finite number of values representable in a computer and sooner or later the loop will terminate. However, the output is implementation dependent, since it is determined by the way reals are stored in the computer.

21. a. HELLO
       HELLO
       HELLO
       HELLO
       GOOD-BYE

    b. HELLO
       GOOD-BYE
       HELLO
       GOOD-BYE
       HELLO
       GOOD-BYE
       HELLO
       GOOD-BYE

22. No difference.

23. No difference.

24. No difference.

THE GOTO STATEMENT

1. These statements will repeat an infinite number of times. In reality, multiuser operating systems usually provide some protection from endless programs. For example, they may set a limit on the total amount of computer time spent by each program.

2. Here is the statement part of a simpler endless program:

```
BEGIN
    1: GOTO 1
END
```

It would be difficult to beat it!

3. Yes, indeed. A statement immediately preceded by a GOTO statement can never be executed unless it is labeled.

4. A program with a patch looks like this.

```
        .
        .
        .
    GOTO 20;
10:     .
        .
        .
    GOTO 30;
20:     .
        .
        .
    GOTO 10
30: END.
```

The patch itself consists of all statements from the statement labeled 20 the statement GOTO 10. Programs with several patches are totally unreadable. They are called *spaghetti* programs.

5. Invalid.

6. Valid.

7. Invalid.

8. Valid.

9. The following two structures will do the same job.

```
FOR COUNTER := INITIAL TO FINAL
DO <statement>
```

and

```
    COUNTER := INITIAL;
10: IF COUNTER <= FINAL
        THEN BEGIN
                <statement>;
                COUNTER := COUNTER + 1;
                GOTO 10
            END
```

10. The following two structures will do the same job.

```
WHILE <boolean expression>
DO <statement>
```

and

```
10: IF <boolean expression>
        THEN BEGIN
                <statement>;
                GOTO 10
            END
```

11. The following two structures will do the same job.

```
REPEAT
    <statement>
UNTIL <boolean expression>
```

and

```
10: <statement>
    IF NOT <boolean expression>
        THEN GOTO 10
```

12. You are right! This is a practical joke.

13.
```
SUM := 0;
I := 1;
REPEAT
```

```
      SUM := SUM + SQR (3 * I);
      I := I + 1
   UNTIL (I > 100) OR (SUM > 200);
   WRITELN (SUM)


14. H := 0;
    K := 3;
    L := 4;
    I := 1;
    J := 2;
    M := 5;
    N := 6


15. IF (NUMBER <> 1) OR (NUMBER <> 2) OR (NUMBER <> 3)
       THEN A := 400
       ELSE
            CASE NUMBER OF
               1:    A := 100;
               2:    A := 200;
               3:    A := 300
            END;
    WRITELN (A)
```

14 Program Structure: Solutions

FUNCTIONS

1. The function returns the Boolean value TRUE if the argument is an even number and FALSE if it is odd.

```
PROGRAM ALPHABET (INPUT, OUTPUT);
{ THIS PROGRAM DETERMINES IF THE ENTERED LETTER IS A VOWEL
   OR A CONSONANT }
VAR
    LETTER : CHAR;
FUNCTION VOWEL (LET : CHAR) : BOOLEAN;
BEGIN
    IF (LET IN ['A', 'E', 'I', 'O', 'U', 'Y'])
        THEN VOWEL := TRUE
        ELSE VOWEL := FALSE
END; { OF FUNCTION }
BEGIN { OF MAIN PROGRAM }
    WRITELN (PLEASE, ENTER A LETTER');
    READLN (LETTER);
    { THE FOLLOWING VERIFIES THAT THE ENTERED CHARACTER IS
        A LETTER }
    IF (ORD (LETTER) >= ORD ('A')) AND (ORD (LETTER) <= ORD
        ('Z'))
        THEN IF VOWEL (LETTER)
```

```
                    THEN WRITELN (LETTER,' IS A VOWEL')
                    ELSE WRITELN (LETTER,' IS A CONSONANT')
             ELSE WRITELN (LETTER,' IS NOT A LETTER')
        END. { OF MAIN PROGRAM }


3.   PROGRAM DISTANCE (INPUT, OUTPUT);
     { THIS PROGRAM COMPUTES THE DISTANCE BETWEEN TWO POINTS }
     VAR
         X1, Y1, Z1, X2, Y2, Z2 : REAL;
     FUNCTION D (A1, B1, C1, A2, B2, C2 : REAL) : REAL;
        BEGIN
              D := SQRT (SQR (A1 - A2) + SQR (B1 - B2) + SQR
                 (C1 - C2))
        END; { OF FUNCTION }
     BEGIN { OF MAIN PROGRAM }
        WRITELN ('PLEASE, ENTER THE COORDINATES OF THE FIRST
                 POINT');
        READLN (X1, Y1, Z1);
        WRITELN ('PLEASE, ENTER THE COORDINATES OF THE SECOND
                 POINT');
        READLN (X2, Y2, Z2);
        WRITELN ('THE DISTANCE IS ',D (X1, Y1, Z1, X2, Y2, Z2)
     END. { OF MAIN PROGRAM }
```

4. All statements may appear except statement f. In statement f the function has only one argument.

5. No, it may appear only in the body of the function.

6. Yes, it may.

7. No difference whatsoever.

8. No value is assigned to the function.

9. The number of actual parameters does not agree with the number of formal parameters.

10. The type of the second actual parameter does not agree with the type the second formal parameter.

11. No, a value must be assigned to the function identifier.

12.   a. 1
         b. -1
         c. 7

13. That declaration is perfectly valid but confusing. It overrides the conventional definition of the EXP function. A will be assigned 0.0.

14. No.

15. Yes, it may. For example, a function returning current time may not have any parameters.

16. The foregoing function heading is invalid. Each parameter in the formal parameter list is the name of a memory location and, therefore, must be unique.

17. Yes, it may. The current values of B, C, and A (in that order) will be assigned to A, B and C (in that order).

18. The order of the actual parameters in each reference to the function must be reversed.

19. Yes, that is legal.

20. Yes, provided that the types ARRAY and RECORD have been defined.

21. No. After control has been transferred back to the calling block, the values of all variables are not retained.

22. Yes, it may.

23. Yes in a, c, e and f. No in b and d.

PROCEDURES

1. A procedure because there are two output parameters. Of course, it is always possible to use two functions, one for the radius and the other for the angle, but the use of a procedure would be more natural.

2. No, because no value is assigned to the procedure identifier.

3. No, not always. Some parameters can serve as both input and output parameters. This is especially common in procedures carrying out successive approximations or iterations. In many cases such procedures take the results of the previous iteration as their input parameters, modify the values and assign them to the same parameters.

4. The program encodes a string by using the following substitution code: A becomes D, B becomes E, C becomes F, etc., X becomes A, Y becomes B and Z becomes C.

5. Here are the major steps.

   • declare a variable, KEY, of the following type:

TYPE TYPEOFKEY = PACKED ARRAY [1..26] OF CHAR;

- assign an arbitrary string of 26 characters (with no character occurring more than once) to KEY.
- for each character of input string, find the value of the subscript of the same character in KEY. This can be done using a REPEAT loop.
- if the value of the subscript is odd, the character is replaced by the next character in KEY. Otherwise it is replaced by the previous character in KEY.

6 It is illegal to assign a value to the identifier of a procedure.

7. The type of X must have been declared before the procedure heading. Then we may refer to the type name inside the heading.

8. Yes. For example, a procedure may print a fixed pattern of characters forming a square. Such a procedure needs no parameters.

9. The types of the formal parameter and the actual one are different.

10. The number of formal parameters differs from the number of actual ones.

11. The first parameter of SECRET3 is a variable parameter. Therefore, the first actual parameter in the procedure call may not be a constant.

12. The second parameter of SECRET4 is a variable parameter. Therefore, the second actual parameter in the procedure call may not be an expression.

13. This line will be printed:

    1   102   3

    Note that A and C are global parameters whereas B is redeclared within the procedure.

14.   3   −1

15.   1   2

16.   1   −1

17.   3   4

18. C and D are value parameters. A, B and E are variable parameters.

19. In the first call, A must be a variable of the type CHAR. Its current value is assigned

to X when the procedure is invoked. In the second call, the character 'A' is assigned to X when the procedure is invoked.

20. Let us consider the following two procedures:

```
PROC1 (VAR A : INTEGER);
BEGIN
    A := 2 * A
END;
```

and

```
PROC2 (A : INTEGER);
BEGIN
    A := 2 * A
END;
```

If the main program includes the following program segment:

```
B := 1;
PROC1 (B);
WRITELN (B)
```

the output will be 2. However, if the main program includes this program segment:

```
B := 1;
PROC2 (B);
WRITELN (B)
```

the output will be 1.

BLOCK STRUCTURE AND SCOPE

```
1. PROGRAM A ...
      .
      .
      .
   PROCEDURE B ...
         .
         .
         .
      BEGIN { OF B }
         .
         .
         .
      END; { OF B }
   PROCEDURE C ...
         .
```

```
                    .
                    .
          BEGIN { OF C }
                    .
                    .
                    .
          END; { OF C }
      BEGIN { OF A }
              .
              .
              .
      END. { OF A }
```

2. Yes, it may.

3. Yes, it may.

4. **PROGRAM A ...**
```
                .
                .
                .
          FUNCTION B ...
                    .
                    .
                    .
              FUNCTION C ...
                        .
                        .
                        .
                  BEGIN { OF C }
                        .
                        .
                        .
                  END; { OF C }
              BEGIN { OF B }
                    .
                    .
                    .
                  END; { OF B }
          BEGIN { OF A }
                .
                .
                .
          END. { OF A }
```

5. No, the variable K is redeclared in B. The memory location associated with K in B is different from the memory location associated with K in A.

6. Yes, the scope of the identifier L declared in B is B, C and D.

7. The one assigned in B.

8. No, it is not. S in C and S in D are different variables.

9. No, it is not. The R that is available in D is the one declared in B.

10. No, it is not. R is a local variable.

11. No, it may not.

12. Yes, it may.

13. Yes, it may.

14. It may only if a FORWARD declaration is used.

15. To statement 1.

16. This is a syntax error because there is no statement labeled 10 within the function SECONDFUNCTION.

17. To statement 2.

18. This is a syntax error because there is no statement labeled 10 within the main program.

19. This is a syntax error: the statement labeled 10 is not unique within its scope.

20. To statement 2.

21. It is illegal to jump from the main program into the middle of a function.

22. **PROGRAM X ...**
    .
    .
    .
    PROCEDURE Z (...); FORWARD;
    PROCEDURE Y ...
       .
       .
       .

```
    BEGIN { OF Y }
           .
           .
           .
      END; { OF Y }
    PROCEDURE Z;
           .
           .
           .
      BEGIN { OF Z }
           .
           .
           .
      END; { OF Z }
    BEGIN { OF X }
           .
           .
           .
    END. { OF X }
```

23. No.

24. No.

25. Yes.

26. Yes.

27. No.

28. No.

29. Yes, this is called mutual recursion.

30. Yes, this is called direct recursion.

31. PROGRAM RECURSIVE1 (INPUT, OUTPUT);
    { THIS PROGRAM COMPUTES THE PRODUCT OF INTEGER
       NUMBERS RECURSIVELY }
    TYPE
       FIVENUMBERS = ARRAY [1..5] OF INTEGER;
    VAR
       FACTORS : FIVENUMBERS;
       COUNTER : INTEGER;

```
FUNCTION PRODUCT (A : FIVENUMBERS; N : INTEGER) : INTEGER;
BEGIN
    IF N = 1
        THEN PRODUCT := A [1]
        ELSE PRODUCT := A [N] * PRODUCT (A, N-1)
END; { OF FUNCTION PRODUCT }
BEGIN { OF MAIN PROGRAM }
    WRITELN ('PLEASE, ENTER 5 INTEGER NUMBERS');
    FOR COUNTER := 1 TO 5
    DO READLN (FACTORS [COUNTER]);
    WRITELN ('THE PRODUCT IS ', PRODUCT (FACTORS, 5))
END. { OF MAIN PROGRAM }
```

Here is how it works:

1. The main program gets to the second WRITELN statement and invokes the function with the parameters (FACTORS, 5).

2. Since N < > 1, the function is to be computed as follows:

```
PRODUCT := A [5] * PRODUCT (A, 4)
```

This assignment cannot be completed until PRODUCT (A, 4) is evaluated.

3. The function PRODUCT is called with parameters (A, 4). PRODUCT is to be computed as follows:

```
PRODUCT := A [4] * PRODUCT (A, 3)
```

4. PRODUCT is called again with parameters (A, 3).

```
PRODUCT := A [3] * PRODUCT (A, 2)
```

5. PRODUCT is called with parameters (A, 2).

```
PRODUCT := A [2] * PRODUCT (A, 1)
```

6. PRODUCT is called with parameters (A, 1). Since N = 1 now, PRODUCT will be evaluated as

```
PRODUCT := A [1]
```

7. Now we can complete the assignment left unfinished in step 5, namely

```
PRODUCT := A [2] * A [1]
```

8. Now we can complete the assignment in step 4, namely

```
PRODUCT := A [3] * A [2] * A [1]
```

9. Now we are able to complete the assignment left unfinished in step 3, namely

```
PRODUCT := A [4] * A [3] * A [2] * A [1]
```

10. Finally we are able to complete the assignment left unfinished in step 2:

```
PRODUCT := A [5] * A [4] * A [3] * A [2] * A [1]
```

11. Control is transferred to the main program which completes the WRITELN statement.

32.
```
PROGRAM NONRECURSIVE (INPUT, OUTPUT);
{ THIS PROGRAM COMPUTES THE PRODUCT OF INTEGER
  NUMBERS NONRECURSIVELY }
TYPE
    FIVENUMBERS = ARRAY [1..5] OF INTEGER;
VAR
    FACTORS : FIVENUMBERS;
    COUNTER : INTEGER;
FUNCTION PRODUCT (A : FIVENUMBERS; N : INTEGER)
                         : INTEGER;
    VAR
        I, TEMPORARY : INTEGER;
BEGIN
    TEMPORARY := 1;
    FOR I := 1 TO N
    DO TEMPORARY := TEMPORARY * A [I];
    PRODUCT := TEMPORARY
END; { OF FUNCTION PRODUCT }
BEGIN { OF MAIN PROGRAM }
    WRITELN ('PLEASE, ENTER 5 INTEGER NUMBERS');
    FOR COUNTER := 1 TO 5
    DO READLN (FACTORS [COUNTER]);
    WRITELN ('THE PRODUCT IS ', PRODUCT (FACTORS,
                                     5))
END. { OF MAIN PROGRAM }
```

Note that the variable TEMPORARY has been introduced due to the fact that the loop

```
PRODUCT := 1;
FOR I := 1 TO N
DO PRODUCT := PRODUCT * A [I]
```

would result in a recursive call.

33. A recursive procedure can be based on the following idea. If the procedure is in-voked when the number of elements of the array is greater than two, the procedure compares the last element with the maximum of all elements of the array except the last one. This comparison can be made with one IF statement. If the procedure is invoked when the number of elements is equal to two, it compares the elements directly using an IF statement.

34. Here is the body of the procedure (the notations are self-explanatory).

```
MAXIMUM := -1.0E10;
{ THIS CONSTANT IS IMPLEMENTATION DEPENDENT.   INITIALLY
  WE ASSIGN
  THE LARGEST NEGATIVE VALUE TO MAXIMUM   }
FOR COUNTER := 1 TO 5
DO IF A [COUNTER] >= MAXIMUM
      THEN BEGIN
                POSITION := COUNTER;
                MAXIMUM := A [COUNTER]
            END
```

15　Intermediate Data Types: Solutions

USER-DEFINED ORDINAL TYPES

1. TYPE
        SPECTRUM = (RED, ORANGE, YELLOW, GREEN, BLUE,
                    INDIGO, VIOLET);
   VAR
        COLOR : SPECTRUM;

2. No. The constant definition part precedes the type definition part.

3. a. 0
   b. 6
   c. ORANGE
   d. BLUE
   e. YELLOW
   f. ORANGE
   g. undefined
   h. undefined

4. VAR
        COLOR : (RED, ORANGE, YELLOW, GREEN, BLUE,
        INDIGO, VIOLET);

5. No, it is not valid. If it were valid, we would be unable to decide, for example, whether ORD ('E') – ORD ('A') is 1, as they are consecutive vowels, or it is 4, as they are characters as well.

6. Let us introduce an array of strings as follows:

```
TYPE
    STRING = PACKED ARRAY [1..3] OF CHAR;
    TYPEOFMONTHNAMES = ARRAY [MONTHTYPE] OF STRING;
VAR
    MONTHNAMES : TYPEOFMONTHNAMES;
```

and make these assignments:

```
MONTHNAMES [JAN] := 'JAN';
MONTHNAMES [FEB] := 'FEB';
MONTHNAMES [MAR] := 'MAR';
MONTHNAMES [APR] := 'APR';
MONTHNAMES [MAY] := 'MAY';
MONTHNAMES [JUN] := 'JUN';
MONTHNAMES [JUL] := 'JUL';
MONTHNAMES [AUG] := 'AUG';
MONTHNAMES [SEP] := 'SEP';
MONTHNAMES [OCT] := 'OCT';
MONTHNAMES [NOV] := 'NOV';
MONTHNAMES [DEC] := 'DEC';
```

Then we can write the value of MONTH by using MONTH as the subscript of the array MONTHNAMES:

```
WRITE (MONTHNAMES [MONTH])
```

7. An alternate solution to the problem is to write a procedure with MONTH as the sole parameter and only one statement:

```
CASE MONTH OF
    JAN : WRITE ('JAN');
    FEB : WRITE ('FEB');
    MAR : WRITE ('MAR');
    APR : WRITE ('APR');
    MAY : WRITE ('MAY');
    JUN : WRITE ('JUN');
    JUL : WRITE ('JUL');
    AUG : WRITE ('AUG');
```

```
      SEP : WRITE ('SEP');
      OCT : WRITE ('OCT');
      NOV : WRITE ('NOV');
      DEC : WRITE ('DEC')
END
```

When this procedure is invoked, it writes the value of the variable MONTH.

8. We shall use the variable STATES declared below as an example.

```
TYPE
    TYPEOFSTATES = (CA, OR, WA, NV, NM, AZ);
VAR
    STATES : TYPEOFSTATES;
```

If we want to assign the value corresponding to a given position, POS, we can use this loop:

```
FOR I := CA TO AZ
DO IF ORD (I) = POS
      THEN STATES := I
```

Here I is a variable of the type TYPEOFSTATES.

9. Yes, subranges of the types CHAR and INTEGER can be arguments of the procedures READ, READLN, WRITE and WRITELN.

10. a. Valid only if MAX is an integer constant defined in the constant definition section and greater than or equal to 10.
   b. Valid
   c. Invalid
   d. Invalid: a bound may not be a function call.
   e. Invalid: subranges are defined for ordinal types only.
   f. Valid
   g. Invalid: 1 and '5' are of different types.

11. b, c and d are correct.
   a, e, f, g and h are incorrect.

12. a. Valid
   b. A run-time error may occur
   c. Valid
   d. Valid

ARRAYS AND STRINGS

1. a. A [1], A[2], A[3], A[4], A[5], A[6], A[7], A[8], A[9], A[10].
   b. B [-5], B [-4], B [-3], B [-2], B [-1], B [0].
   c. C ['N'], C ['O'], C ['P'], C ['R'].
   d. POPULATION [CA]
      POPULATION [OR]
      POPULATION [WA]
   e. E [3, -2], E [3, -1], E [3, 0]
      E [4, -2], E [4, -1], E [4, 0]
      E [5, -2], E [5, -1], E [5, 0]
   f. SEATS [1,'A'], SEATS [1,'B'], SEATS [1,'C']
      SEATS [2,'A'], SEATS [2,'B'], SEATS [2,'C']
      SEATS [3,'A'], SEATS [3,'B'], SEATS [3,'C']
   g. VERTICES [0, 0, 0], VERTICES [0, 0, 1]
      VERTICES [0, 1, 0], VERTICES [0, 1, 1]
      VERTICES [1, 0, 0], VERTICES [1, 0, 1]
      VERTICES [1, 1, 0], VERTICES [1, 1, 1]
   h. RESPONSE [TRUE, TRUE], RESPONSE [TRUE, FALSE]
      RESPONSE [FALSE, TRUE], RESPONSE [FALSE, FALSE]
   i. I [TRUE, X], I [TRUE, Y], I [TRUE, Z]
      I [FALSE, X], I [FALSE, Y], I [FALSE, Z]

2. a. VAR
         A : ARRAY [1..10] OF INTEGER;
   b. VAR
         B : ARRAY [-5..0] OF CHAR;
   c. VAR
         C : ARRAY ['N'..'R'] OF REAL;
   d. TYPE
         STATES = (CA, OR, WA, NV, NM, AZ);
      VAR
         POPULATION : ARRAY [CA..WA] OF INTEGER;
   e. VAR
         E : ARRAY [3..5, -2..0] OF CHAR;
   f. VAR
         SEATS : ARRAY [1..3, 'A'..'C'] OF BOOLEAN;
   g. VAR
         VERTICES : ARRAY [0..1, 0..1, 0..1] OF BOOLEAN;
   h. VAR
         RESPONSE : ARRAY [BOOLEAN, BOOLEAN] OF BOOLEAN;
   i. TYPE
         A = (X, Y, Z);

```
VAR
    I : ARRAY [BOOLEAN, A] OF CHAR;
```

3. a. Valid only if MAX is an integer constant defined in the constant definition section and greater than or equal to -1.
   b. Valid
   c. Invalid
   d. Invalid: a bound may not be a function call.
   e. Invalid: a subscript may not be real.
   f. Valid
   g. Invalid: 1 and '5' have different types.
   h. Valid
   i. Invalid: this definition would create an infinite array.
   j. Valid.

4. Assuming that the two arrays have been declared as follows:

```
TYPE
    TYPEOFNUMBERS = ARRAY [1..100] OF REAL;
    TYPEOFDIFFERENCES = ARRAY [1..99] OF REAL;
VAR
    NUMBERS : TYPEOFNUMBERS;
    DIFFERENCES : TYPEOFDIFFERENCES;
```

and COUNTER is integer, the following statement will solve the problem:

```
FOR COUNTER := 1 TO 99
DO DIFFERENCES [COUNTER] := NUMBERS [COUNTER + 1]
                              - NUMBERS [COUNTER]
```

5. All of them are valid.

6. Declare an array, GRID, as follows:

```
TYPE
    STATE = (EMPTY, X, O);
    GRIDTYPE = ARRAY [1..3, 1..3] OF STATE;
VAR
    GRID : GRIDTYPE;
```

Introduce a Boolean variable, PLAYER, alternating its value after each move. If it equals TRUE, the next move is interpreted as a cross, otherwise it is a circle.
   Initialize GRID as follows:

```
FOR I := 1 TO 3
DO FOR J := 1 TO 3
    DO GRID ⌈I, J] := EMPTY;
```

The program solicits a move and verifies that the appropriate element of the array GRID is empty. Then it checks if the current move results in a winning combination. If not, it solicits the next move. It is worthwhile to organize the checking as a separate subroutine.

7.
```
PROGRAM MEAN (INPUT, OUTPUT);
CONST
    MAX = 10;
TYPE
    TYPEOFNUMBERS = ARRAY [1..MAX] OF REAL;
VAR
    NUMBERS : TYPEOFNUMBERS;
    MEAN, STDEV : REAL;
    COUNTER : INTEGER;
BEGIN
    FOR COUNTER := 1 TO MAX
    DO BEGIN
            WRITELN ('PLEASE, ENTER A NUMBER');
            READLN (NUMBERS [COUNTER])
        END;
    MEAN := 0;
    STDEV := 0;
    FOR COUNTER := 1 TO MAX
    DO BEGIN
            MEAN := MEAN + NUMBERS [COUNTER];
            STDEV := STDEV + SQR (NUMBERS [COUNTER])
        END;
    {We are using the fact that the square of the

    standard deviation
    is the mean of the squares minus the square of the
    mean}
    MEAN := MEAN / MAX;
    STDEV := SQRT (STDEV / MAX - SQR (MEAN));
    WRITELN ('THE MEAN IS ', MEAN);
    WRITELN ('THE STANDARD DEVIATION IS ', STDEV)
END.
```

8. Suppose that the array has been declared as follows:

    TYPE

```
      TYPEOFNUMBERS = ARRAY [MINROW..MAXROW, MINCOLUMN..
                            MAXCOLUMN] OF REAL;
    VAR
        NUMBERS : TYPEOFNUMBERS;
```

and all necessary variables have been declared appropriately. I shall consider the first version only. The other two versions are left to you.

```
MAXIMUM := NUMBERS [1, 1] - 1;
MINIMUM := NUMBERS [1, 1] + 1;
FOR ROW := MINROW TO MAXROW
DO FOR COLUMN := MINCOLUMN TO MAXCOLUMN
    DO BEGIN
            IF NUMBERS [ROW, COLUMN] > MAXIMUM
                THEN BEGIN
                        MAXIMUM := NUMBERS [ROW, COLUMN];
                        ROW1 := ROW;
                        COLUMN1 := COLUMN
                    END;
            IF NUMBERS [ROW, COLUMN] < MINIMUM
                THEN BEGIN
                        MINIMUM := NUMBERS [ROW, COLUMN];
                        ROW2 := ROW;
                        COLUMN2 := COLUMN
                    END
        END;
WRITELN ('MAXIMUM IS ', MAXIMUM,' ITS POSITION IS ',ROW1,
        COLUMN1);
WRITELN ('MINIMUM IS ', MINIMUM,' ITS POSITION IS ',ROW2,
        COLUMN2)
END.
```

10. A solution to this problem can be obtained as a by-product of a solution to the sorting problem; see Chapter 8.

11. Yes, it can. For instance, if A is an array and P is a procedure, the procedure can be called as

```
P (A)
```

12. The answer depends on how A and B were declared. If they were declared with the same type, for instance

```
TYPE
    TYPEOFAANDB = ARRAY [1..100] OF REAL;
VAR
    A, B : TYPEOFAANDB;
```

then the assignment statement above is valid. If they were declared with equivalent but not identical types, such as

```
TYPE
    TYPEOFA = ARRAY [1..100] OF REAL;
    TYPEOFB = ARRAY [1..100] OF REAL;
VAR
    A : TYPEOFA;
    B : TYPEOFB;
```

then the assignment above is invalid. If A and B were declared without naming a type, for instance

```
VAR
    A : ARRAY [1..100] OF REAL;
    B : ARRAY [1..100] OF REAL;
```

then the assignment statement is invalid.

13. Assuming that all variables below have been declared properly, here is a simple, although not economical, solution:

```
FLAG := TRUE;
FOR ROW := 1 TO N
DO FOR COLUMN := 1 TO ROW - 1
    DO IF A [ROW, COLUMN] <> A [COLUMN, ROW]
            THEN FLAG := FALSE;
IF FLAG
    THEN WRITELN ('THE MATRIX IS SYMMETRICAL')
    ELSE WRITELN ('THE MATRIX IS NOT SYMMETRICAL')
```

14. Use an algorithm known as the Sieve of Eratosthenes. According to this algorithm, we start with the array of 1000 integer numbers and successively remove all numbers divisible by two but two, all numbers divisible by three but three, and so on. Eventually this algorithm removes all composite numbers.

15. a. Incorrect. Although generally speaking packed arrays occupy less memory than their unpacked counterparts, the amount of savings is computer dependent.

Some compilers simply ignore the word PACKED.

    b. Correct.

    c. Incorrect. Any array can be packed but in practice packing is applied to Boolean arrays and arrays of characters. Note that other structured types, such as records, can be packed, too.

    d. Incorrect.

16. It can be argument of WRITE and WRITELN but not READ or READLN. Some implementations define extended versions of Pascal that allow a string variable be an argument of all four procedures.

17. a. Invalid because the string on the right side of the assignment operator consists of fewer than 10 characters.

    b. Valid.

    c. Invalid because the string on the right side of the assignment operator is more than 10 characters long.

18.
```
PROGRAM BACKWARD (INPUT, OUTPUT);
CONST
    LENGTH = 10;
TYPE
    STRING = PACKED ARRAY [1..LENGTH] OF CHAR;
VAR
    WORD : STRING;
    COUNTER : INTEGER;
BEGIN
    WRITELN ('PLEASE, ENTER A TEN LETTER WORD');
    FOR COUNTER := LENGTH DOWNTO 1
    DO READ (WORD [COUNTER]);
    WRITELN ('THE WORD WRITTEN IN THE REVERSE
                ORDER IS ',WORD)
END.
```

SETS

1.
```
TYPE
    LISTOFHOBBIES = (HIKING, MOVIE GOING,
                        READING, TABLE TENNIS,
                        MUSIC, POLITICS);
    TYPEOFHOBBIES = SET OF LISTOFHOBBIES;
VAR
    HOBBIES : TYPEOFHOBBIES;
```

2. 16 values:

```
[]
[LIVINGROOM]
[DININGROOM]
[BEDROOM]
[KITCHEN]
[LIVINGROOM, DININGROOM]
[LIVINGROOM, BEDROOM]
[LIVINGROOM, KITCHEN]
[DININGROOM, BEDROOM]
[DININGROOM, KITCHEN]
[BEDROOM, KITCHEN]
[LIVINGROOM, DININGROOM, BEDROOM]
[LIVINGROOM, DININGROOM, KITCHEN]
[LIVINGROOM, BEDROOM, KITCHEN]
[DININGROOM, BEDROOM, KITCHEN]
[LIVINGROOM, DININGROOM, BEDROOM, KITCHEN]
```

3. The base type of a set must be an ordinal type.

4. This set would be infinite while every implementation restricts the size of the base type. We can use a subrange of the type INTEGER as the base type for a set. To wit, this definition:

```
TYPE
    A = 30..40;
    B = SET OF A;
```

is absolutely acceptable.

5. a. `['A', 'C', 'D', 'E', 'F', 'G', 'H', 'U']`
   b. `['F']`
   c. `['A', 'C', 'U']`
   d. `['F', 'M', 'P', 'C']`
   e. `['C', 'F']`
   f. `[]`
   g. `[]`

6. a. TRUE
   b. TRUE
   c. FALSE
   d. FALSE
   e. FALSE

7. TRUE

8. The expression is invalid, for the relational operator $<$ is not defined with sets.

9. ```
NUMBER := 0;
FOR COUNTER := CA TO AZ
DO IF COUNTER IN STATES
        THEN NUMBER := NUMBER + 1
```

10. Set union is defined only when both operands are sets. Hence, the correct form of this statement is

```
HOBBIES := HOBBIES + [MUSIC]
```

11. No. The constant definition part must precede the type definition part.

12. Yes.

13. For the sake of simplicity, let us assume that all hobbies are coded by integer numbers from 1 to 30. Each person will enter a list of hobbies followed by a sentinel number, say -1, to indicate the end of the list.

```
PROGRAM COMPATIBILITY (INPUT, OUTPUT);
CONST
    MIN = 3;
TYPE
    RANGE = 1..30;
    HOBBIES = SET OF RANGE;
VAR
    HOBBIES1, HOBBIES2 : HOBBIES;
    NUMBER, COUNTER : INTEGER;
BEGIN
    {Initialize both sets}
    HOBBIES1 := [];
    HOBBIES2 := [];
    COUNTER := 0;
    {Read the first set}
    WRITELN ('PLEASE, ENTER THE FIRST GROUP OF HOBBIES');
    READLN (NUMBER);
    WHILE NUMBER <> -1
    DO BEGIN
            HOBBIES1 := HOBBIES1 + [NUMBER];
            WRITELN ('ENTER NEXT HOBBY');
            READLN (NUMBER)
        END;
    {Read the second set}
```
```

```
            WRITELN ('PLEASE, ENTER THE SECOND GROUP OF HOBBIES');
            READLN (NUMBER);
            WHILE NUMBER <> -1
            DO BEGIN
                   HOBBIES2 := HOBBIES2 + [NUMBER];
                   WRITELN ('ENTER NEXT HOBBY');
                   READLN (NUMBER)
               END;
            {Compute the number of elements in the intersection}
            FOR NUMBER := 1 TO 30
            DO IF NUMBER IN (HOBBIES1 * HOBBIES2)
                   THEN COUNTER := COUNTER + 1;
            IF COUNTER <= MIN
               THEN WRITELN ('YOU ARE COMPATIBLE')
               ELSE WRITELN ('YOU ARE NOT COMPATIBLE')
        END.
```

14. a. From the greater of the two numbers, M and N, to M + N.
    b. From 0 to the lesser of the two numbers, M and N.
    c. From 0 to M.

15.
```
IF A IN [3..6, 8]
    THEN <statement 1>
    ELSE <statement 2>
```

16. Let us use abbreviations for the sake of brevity. Here are the definitions and declarations:

```
TYPE
    VEGETABLES = (ART, ASP, BEA, BRO, EGG, TOM);
    FARMING = SET OF VEGETABLES;
    STATES = (CA, OR, WA, NV, NM, AZ);
    STATEFARMING = ARRAY [STATES] OF FARMING;
VAR
    AGRICULTURE : STATEFARMING;
```

We can use the following statements to initialize the array AGRICULTURE:

```
AGRICULTURE [CA] := [ART, ASP, EGG];
AGRICULTURE [OR] := [BEA, BRO, EGG];
AGRICULTURE [WA] := [BEA, BRO, TOM];
AGRICULTURE [NV] := [BEA, TOM];
AGRICULTURE [NM] := [ART];
AGRICULTURE [AZ] := [ASP];
```

17. Introduce two arrays of strings: one for the vegetables and the other for the states. Then test for membership in every set using IN and output appropriate strings.

FILES

1. a. Yes
   b. Yes
   c. No
   d. Yes

2. Not important at all.

3. No, it can be a text file, too. If it is a text file, the statement WRITE (F,X) will write a sequence of characters denoting X to file F.

4. Yes, it may.

5. No, the WRITELN and READLN statements are used only with text files because only text files are composed of lines.

6. The file OUTPUT.

7. A WRITE statement may not follow a READ statement. The file must be rewritten first.

8. No. INPUT is a special file and data can only be read from it.

9. It depends on the declaration part. X can be the identifier of a file or of a variable but not both.

10. Yes, but only as a variable parameter. This convention has been made to avoid time and memory consuming copying of files.

11. No, it is not valid.

12.
```
PROGRAM TRUNCATE (OLDFILE, NEWFILE, OUTPUT);
{This program creates NewFile by truncating
OldFile}
CONST
    LINELIMIT = 100;
VAR
    OLDFILE, NEWFILE : TEXT;
    C : CHAR;
    COUNTER : INTEGER;
BEGIN
    RESET (OLDFILE);
```

```
        REWRITE (NEWFILE);
        COUNTER := 1;
        WHILE NOT EOF (OLDFILE) AND (COUNTER <= LINELIMIT)
        DO BEGIN
                WHILE NOT EOLN (OLDFILE)
                DO BEGIN
                        READ (OLDFILE, C);
                        WRITE (NEWFILE, C)
                    END;
                READLN (OLDFILE);
                WRITELN (NEWFILE);
                COUNTER := COUNTER + 1
            END
    END.
```

13.
```
    PROGRAM ODD (OLDFILE, NEWFILE, OUTPUT);
    {This program copies only odd-numbered lines from OldFile
     to NewFile}
    VAR
        OLDFILE, NEWFILE : TEXT;
        C : CHAR;
    BEGIN
        RESET (OLDFILE);
        REWRITE (NEWFILE);
        WHILE NOT EOF (OLDFILE)
        DO BEGIN
                WHILE NOT EOLN (OLDFILE)
                DO BEGIN
                        READ (OLDFILE, C);
                        WRITE (NEWFILE, C)
                    END;
                READLN (OLDFILE);
                READLN (OLDFILE);
                WRITELN (NEWFILE)
            END
    END.
```

14.
```
    PROGRAM COMPARE (FILE1, FILE2, OUTPUT);
    {This program determines whether File1 and File2 are
    identical files of integers}
    TYPE
        INTFILE = FILE OF INTEGER;
    VAR
        FILE1, FILE2 : INTFILE;
```

```
      NUMBER1, NUMBER2 : INTEGER;
      FLAG : BOOLEAN;
   BEGIN
      RESET (FILE1);
      RESET (FILE2);
      FLAG := TRUE;
      WHILE NOT EOF (FILE1) AND NOT EOF (FILE2) AND FLAG = TRUE
      DO BEGIN
            READ (FILE1, NUMBER1);
            READ (FILE2, NUMBER2);
            IF NUMBER1 <> NUMBER2
               THEN FLAG := FALSE
         END;
   {We could get out of the previous loop for one of the three
    reasons:
     1.  Two different numbers were encountered.
     2.  Both end-of-files were reached simultaneously.
     3.  Only one end-of-file was reached.
    Now is the time to find out which reason took place}
      IF FLAG AND EOF (FILE1) AND EOF (FILE2)
         THEN WRITELN ('THE FILES ARE IDENTICAL')
         ELSE WRITELN ('THE FILES ARE NOT IDENTICAL')
   END.
```

15.
```
   PROGRAM CONCATENATE (FIRST, SECOND, RESULT, OUTPUT);
   {This program creates the file RESULT by appending the
    file SECOND to the end of the file FIRST}
   TYPE
      REALFILE = FILE OF REAL;
   VAR
      FIRST, SECOND, RESULT : REALFILE;
      NUMBER : REAL;
   BEGIN
      REWRITE (RESULT);
      RESET (FIRST);
      WHILE NOT EOF (FIRST)
      DO BEGIN
            READ (FIRST, NUMBER);
            WRITE (RESULT, NUMBER)
         END;
      RESET (SECOND);
      WHILE NOT EOF (SECOND)
      DO BEGIN
            READ (SECOND, NUMBER);
```

```
            WRITE (RESULT, NUMBER)
        END
    END.
```

16. Copy the old file to the new one, character by character, until you encounter the first suspicious character—a letter after a blank or at the beginning of a line. At this point the copying is suspended and this and following characters are accumulated in an array. If this group of characters happens to be a four letter word, the group is discarded and the copying is resumed. Otherwise, the group is copied to the new file.

A character, C, is a letter if the Boolean expression

```
(ORD (C) >= ORD ('A')) AND (ORD (C) <= ORD ('Z'))
```

is TRUE.

17.
```
PROGRAM COUNT (F, OUTPUT);
{This program computes the number of lines and characters
 in a text file}
VAR
    F : TEXT;
    LINES, CHARACTERS : INTEGER;
BEGIN
    RESET (F);
    LINES := 0;
    CHARACTERS := 0;
    WHILE NOT EOF (F)
    DO BEGIN
            LINES := LINES + 1;
            WHILE NOT EOLN (F)
            DO BEGIN
                    GET (F);
                    CHARACTERS := CHARACTERS + 1
                END;
            READLN (F)
        END;
    WRITELN ('THERE ARE ',LINES,' LINES AND ',CHARACTERS,'
            CHARACTERS')
END.
```

18. It is useful to introduce a variable functioning like a finite state machine and controlling the actions to be taken as you read the old file, character by character. The variable can be in one of three states at any given moment. Its state transitions are as follows:

State 1. Start out at state 1. If the current character is not a period, an exclamation point, or a question mark, remain in state 1; otherwise move to state 2. As long as you are in state 1, all characters of the old file are copied to the new file.

State 2. If the current character is not a blank, then return to state 1. Otherwise move to state 3. Whatever the current character, it is copied to the new file.

State 3. If the current character is not a blank, move to state 1. Otherwise remain in state 3. If you do remain in state 3, the current character is not copied to the new file.

This introduction will help you understand the following program.

```
PROGRAM BLANKBUSTER (OLDFILE, NEWFILE, OUTPUT);
{This program removes extra characters after each period,
exclamation point and question mark}
VAR
    OLDFILE, NEWFILE : TEXT;
    C : CHAR;
    STATE : 1..3;
BEGIN
    RESET (OLDFILE);
    REWRITE (NEWFILE);
    STATE := 1;
    WHILE NOT EOF (OLDFILE)
    DO BEGIN
            WHILE NOT EOLN (OLDFILE)
            DO BEGIN
                    READ (OLDFILE, C);
                    CASE STATE OF
                        1 : BEGIN
                                WRITE (NEWFILE, C);
                                IF C IN ['.', '!', '?']
                                    THEN STATE := 2
                            END;
                        2 : BEGIN
                                WRITE (NEWFILE, C);
                                IF C = ' '
                                    THEN STATE := 3
                                    ELSE STATE := 1
                            END;
                        3 : BEGIN
                                IF C <> ' '
                                    THEN BEGIN
                                            WRITE (NEWFILE, C);
                                            STATE := 1
                                        END
                    END
```

```
                    END {of case}
                 END; {of the inner while loop}
                 READLN (OLDFILE);
                 WRITELN (NEWFILE)
           END {of the outer while loop}
      END. {of the program}


19.  PROGRAM CENTER (OLDFILE, NEWFILE, OUTPUT);
     {This program creates NEWFILE by centering all lines of
       OLDFILE}
     CONST
        MAX = 40;
     TYPE
        STRING = PACKED ARRAY [1..MAX] OF CHAR;
     VAR
        OLDFILE, NEWFILE : TEXT;
        LINE : STRING;
        C : CHAR;
        COUNTER1, COUNTER2, SHIFT : INTEGER;
     BEGIN
        RESET (OLDFILE);
        REWRITE (NEWFILE);
        WHILE NOT EOF (OLDFILE)
        DO BEGIN
              COUNTER1 := 0;
              WHILE NOT EOLN (OLDFILE)
              DO BEGIN
                  COUNTER1 := COUNTER1 + 1;
                  READ (OLDFILE, LINE [COUNTER1]
              END;
              IF (COUNTER1 > 0) AND (COUNTER1 < 40)
              THEN BEGIN
                      SHIFT := (MAX - COUNTER1) DIV 2;
                      FOR COUNTER2 := COUNTER1 DOWNTO 1
                      DO STRING [COUNTER2 + SHIFT] :=

                                 STRING [COUNTER2];
                      FOR COUNTER2 := SHIFT DOWNTO 1
                      DO STRING [COUNTER2] := ' '
                   END;
              WRITELN (NEWFILE);
              READLN (OLDFILE)
           END
     END.
```

20. This problem is somewhat similar to problem 16.

21. This problem is also somewhat similar to problem 16.

22. Again this problem is somewhat similar to problem 16.

23.
```
PROGRAM TELEPHONE (DIRECTORY, OUTPUT);
{This program checks if every line of a text
 file is a valid telephone number}
VAR
    DIRECTORY : TEXT;
    C : CHAR;
    COUNTER, LINE : INTEGER;
BEGIN
    RESET (DIRECTORY);
    LINE := 0;
    WHILE NOT EOF (DIRECTORY)
    DO BEGIN
            LINE := LINE + 1;
            COUNTER := 0;
            WHILE NOT EOLN (DIRECTORY) AND
            (COUNTER <= 15)
            DO BEGIN
                    COUNTER := COUNTER + 1;
                    READ (DIRECTORY, C);
                    CASE COUNTER OF
                        1 : IF C <> '('
                                THEN WRITELN ('NO LEFT
                                PAREN IN LINE ',LINE);
                        2, 3, 4, 7, 8, 9, 11, 12, 13,
                        14 :
                            IF (ORD (C) < ORD ('0'))
                                OR (ORD (C) > ORD ('9')
                                )THEN WRITELN ('NOT A
                                DIGIT IN LINE ',LINE);
                        5 : IF C <> ')'
                                THEN WRITELN ('NO RIGHT
                                PAREN IN LINE ',LINE);
                        10: IF C <> '-'
                                THEN WRITELN ('NO DASH
                                IN LINE ',LINE);
                        15: WRITELN ('EXTRA CHARACTERS
                                IN LINE ',LINE)
```

```
                    END;
                    READLN (DIRECTORY)
              END;
         IF COUNTER < 14
         THEN WRITELN ('LINE ',LINE,' IS TOO SHORT')
      END
   END.
```

24.
```
PROGRAM SPLIT (MIXED, OLD, YOUNG, OUTPUT);
{This program splits a text file according to the year
of birth of the people}
CONST
   THRESHOLD = 1942;
VAR
   MIXED, OLD, YOUNG : TEXT;
   NUMBER : INTEGER;
   C : CHARACTER;
BEGIN
   RESET (MIXED);
   REWRITE (OLD);
   REWRITE (YOUNG);
   WHILE NOT EOF (MIXED)
   DO BEGIN
         READ (MIXED, NUMBER);
         IF NUMBER < THRESHOLD
            THEN BEGIN
                    WRITE (OLD, NUMBER);
                    WHILE NOT EOLN (MIXED)
                    DO BEGIN
                          READ (MIXED, C);
                          WRITE (OLD, C)
                       END;
                    WRITELN (OLD)
                 END
            ELSE BEGIN
                    WRITE (YOUNG, NUMBER);
                    WHILE NOT EOLN (MIXED)
                    DO BEGIN
                          READ (MIXED, C);
                          WRITE (YOUNG, C)
                       END;
                    WRITELN (YOUNG)
                 END;
         READLN (MIXED)
      END
   END.
```

25. This program is somewhat like the program in problem 13.

26.
```
PROGRAM INSERT (OLDFILE, NEWFILE, OUTPUT);
{This program inserts an empty line after each
  line of the original text file}
VAR
    OLDFILE, NEWFILE : TEXT;
    C : CHARACTER;
BEGIN
    RESET (OLDFILE);
    REWRITE (NEWFILE);
    WHILE NOT EOF (OLDFILE)
    DO BEGIN
            WHILE NOT EOLN (OLDFILE)
            DO BEGIN
                    READ (OLDFILE, C);
                    WRITE (NEWFILE, C)
                END;
            READLN (OLDFILE);
            WRITELN (NEWFILE);
            WRITELN (NEWFILE)
        END
END.
```

27. This program is somewhat like the program in problem 26.

28.
```
PROGRAM MERGE (NAME, PHONE, BOTH, OUTPUT);
{This program merges corresponding lines of two
  files}
VAR
    NAME, PHONE, BOTH : TEXT;
    C : CHAR;
BEGIN
    RESET (NAME);
    RESET (PHONE);
    REWRITE (BOTH);
    WHILE NOT EOF (NAME) AND NOT EOF (PHONE)
    DO BEGIN
            WHILE NOT EOLN (NAME)
            DO BEGIN
                    READ (NAME, C);
                    WRITE (BOTH, C)
                END;
            WHILE NOT EOLN (PHONE)
            DO BEGIN
```

```
                    READ (PHONE, C);
                    WRITE (BOTH, C)
                END;
            WRITELN (BOTH);
            READLN (NAME);
            READLN (PHONE)
        END;
    {It does not hurt to check if both files reached their ends
    simultaneously}
        IF NOT EOF (NAME) OR NOT EOF (PHONE)
            THEN WRITELN ('FILES ARE OF DIFFERENT LENGTHS')
    END.


29. PROGRAM FREQUENCY (F, OUTPUT);
    {This program computes the frequency distribution of all
    letters in a  text file.  All non-letter characters are
    ignored}
    TYPE
        TYPEOFFREQUENCY = ARRAY ['A'..'Z'] OF REAL;
    VAR
        F : TEXT;
        FREQUENCY : TYPEOFFREQUENCY;
        TOTALSUM : INTEGER;
        C, LETTER : CHAR;
    BEGIN
        {Initialization part}
        RESET (F);
        TOTALSUM := 0;
        FOR LETTER := 'A' TO 'Z'
        DO FREQUENCY [LETTER] := 0;
        {Computing the histogram}
        WHILE NOT EOF (F)
        DO BEGIN
                WHILE NOT EOLN (F)
                DO BEGIN
                    READ (F, C);
                    IF (ORD (C) >= ORD ('A')) AND (ORD (C) <=
                    ORD ('Z'))
                        THEN BEGIN
                                FREQUENCY [C] := FREQUENCY [C]
                                                + 1;
                                TOTALSUM := TOTALSUM + 1
                            END
```

```
            END;
            READLN (F)
        END;
    FOR LETTER := 'A' TO 'Z'
    DO WRITELN ('FREQUENCY OF ',LETTER,' IS ',FREQUENCY
                                [LETTER] / TOTALSUM)
END.
```

16 Records: Solutions

DEFINITIONS AND DECLARATIONS

1. ```
TYPE
    MONTHTYPE = (JANUARY, FEBRUARY, MARCH, APRIL, MAY,
                 JUNE, JULY, AUGUST, SEPTEMBER, OCTOBER,
                 NOVEMBER, DECEMBER);
    DAYTYPE = 1..31;
    DATE = RECORD
               MONTH : MONTHTYPE;
               DAY   : DAYTYPE;
               YEAR : INTEGER
           END;
VAR
    TODAY : DATE;
```

2. The third record type definition is invalid because the field identifier ID is not unique within the record. The other definitions are valid. The same field identifier may be present in several different record types because an individual field is referred to by specifying both the record identifier and the field identifier.

3. We will define an array of records:
```

```
TYPE
    STRING = PACKED ARRAY [1..20] OF CHAR;
    STUDENT = RECORD
                    NAME : STRING;
                    YEAROFBIRTH : INTEGER;
                    UNITS : INTEGER;
                    GPA : REAL
                END;
    CLASS = ARRAY [1..30] OF STUDENT;
VAR
    PHYSICS : CLASS;
```

4. Each class can be described as an array of strings. The entire information can be represented as a record of the arrays:

```
TYPE
    STRING = PACKED ARRAY [1..MAXNAME] OF CHAR;
    CLASS1 = ARRAY [1..MAXCLASS1] OF STRING;
    CLASS2 = ARRAY [1..MAXCLASS2] OF STRING;
    CLASS3 = ARRAY [1..MAXCLASS3] OF STRING;
    CLASSES = RECORD
                    PASCAL : CLASS1;
                    DATABASE : CLASS2;
                    NETWORKS : CLASS3
                END;
VAR
    PROFESSOR : CLASSES;
```

5. ```
TYPE
    STRING = PACKED ARRAY [1..20] OF CHAR;
    CONDITION = RECORD
                    TEMPERATURE : INTEGER;
                    PRESSURE : INTEGER
                END;
    PATIENT   = RECORD
                    NAME : STRING;

                    ROOM : INTEGER;
                    MORNINGCONDITION : CONDITION;
                    AFTERNOONCONDITION : CONDITION
                END;
```

6. The record type B must have been defined before the record type A:
```

```
TYPE
   B = RECORD
           B1 : CHAR;
           B2 : REAL
       END;
   A = RECORD
           A1 : INTEGER;
           A2 : REAL;
           A3 : B
       END;
```

Here is another way of defining the same structure:

```
TYPE
   A = RECORD
           A1 : INTEGER;
           A2 : REAL;
           A3 : RECORD
                   B1 : CHAR;
                   B2 : REAL
                END
       END;
```

While the latter definition is more compact, the former is more flexible because it explicity defines the type B, which can later be used in other definitions.

7.
```
VAR
   BOOK : RECORD
               AUTHOR : PACKED ARRAY [1..30] OF CHAR;
               TITLE  : PACKED ARRAY [1..30] OF CHAR;
               GROUP  : (FICTION, BIOGRAPHY, TEXTBOOK,
                         MANUAL);
               PRICE  : REAL
           END;
```

8. Yes, they are valid and unambiguous.

9. Yes, it may.

10. The answer to all four questions is yes.

11. Yes, it may. If a whole record is used as a parameter, all its fields are passed to the function or the procedure even though they are not explicitly listed in the call.

12. Yes, they are (in the sense that any interchange does not affect any statement ac-

cessing the record X's fields).

13. This statement is invalid. In order to write the value of a record to the file OUT-PUT, the fields must be given as arguments of the procedure WRITE, such as

```
WRITE (CLIENT.NAME, CLIENT.ADDRESS, ...)
```

Only if a file, F, is a file of records, the whole record can be an argument of the procedure WRITE or READ, such as

```
WRITE (F, CLIENT)
```

ACCESS METHODS.

```
1. MYHOUSE.NUMBEROFROOMS := 1;
   MYHOUSE.ADDRESS.STREETADDRESS := '3230 YOSEMITE
   AVENUE';
   MYHOUSE.ADDRESS.CITY := 'EL CERRITO, CA ';
   MYHOUSE.PRICE := 30000
```

2. The following assignments illustrate the rules:

```
F ['X'].B := 3;
F ['Z'].B := 0;
F ['Z'].C := 'Z';
F ['Y'].D := 3.14
```

3. ```
WITH BOOK
DO BEGIN
        AUTHOR := 'WILLIAM SHAKESPEARE';
        TITLE := 'MUCH ADO ABOUT NOTHING';
        GROUP := FICTION;
        PRICE := 4.95
   END
```

4. ```
WITH MYHOUSE, ADDRESS
DO BEGIN
        NUMBEROFROOMS := 1;
        STREETADDRESS := '3230 YOSEMITE AVENUE';
        CITY := 'EL CERRITO, CA ';
        PRICE := 30000
   END
```

```
5. FOR I := 'X' TO 'Z'
   DO WITH F [I]
      DO BEGIN
             B := SQR (ORD (I) - 5);
             C := PRED (PRED (I));
             D := 3.14
         END
```

6. No, they do not have to be nested. If , for example, the records A and B are declared as follows:

```
VAR
   A : RECORD
           M : INTEGER;
           N : REAL
         END;
   B : RECORD
           P : CHAR;
           Q : BOOLEAN
         END;
```

then the statement

```
WITH A, B
DO BEGIN
       M := 5;
       N := 7.4;
       P := CHR (39);
       Q := 2 * 2 = 5
    END
```

is equivalent to

```
A.M := 5;
A.N := 7.4;
B.P := CHR (39);
B.Q := 2 * 2 = 5
```

7. They are equivalent if the records A and B are not nested and if they do not have a field by the same name (at least such a field must not be present in the statement).

8. In this construction, PRICE denotes HOUSE2.PRICE rather than HOUSE1.PRICE because the construction

```
WITH HOUSE1, HOUSE2
DO <statement>
```

is equivalent to

```
WITH HOUSE1
DO WITH HOUSE2
   DO <statement>
```

and by Pascal's rules of nested scopes, the innermost identifier always takes precedence. If it should be necessary to refer to HOUSE1.PRICE within the same structure, its full name, HOUSE1.PRICE, should be used.

9. The notation BOOK [5].AUTHOR implies that BOOK is an array of records, BOOK [5] is an element of the array and BOOK [5].AUTHOR is a field of this element.

On the other hand, the notation BOOK.AUTHOR [5] implies that the field AUTHOR itself is an array (it can be a string, for example) and BOOK.AUTHOR [5] refers to an element of this array.

10. a. legal
    b. and c. are illegal because the value of a record variable can be assigned to another record variable of the same type only. While the types A and B are compatible, they are not the same.

11.
```
PROGRAM STUDENT (INPUT, OUTPUT);
{This program selects student records with GPA
above a given point}
CONST
    CLASSSIZE := 30;
    CUTOFFPOINT := 2.7;
TYPE
    STUDENT = RECORD
                  ID : INTEGER;
                  GPA : REAL
              END;
VAR
    CLASS : ARRAY [1..CLASSSIZE] OF STUDENT;
    COUNTER : INTEGER;
BEGIN
    FOR COUNTER := 1 TO CLASSSIZE
    DO BEGIN
            WRITELN ('PLEASE, ENTER A STUDENT''S
                     ID');
```

```
            READLN (CLASS [COUNTER].ID);
            WRITELN ('NOW ENTER THAT STUDENT''S GPA');
            READLN (CLASS [COUNTER].GPA)
         END;
      FOR COUNTER := 1 TO CLASSSIZE
      DO IF CLASS [COUNTER].GPA > CUTOFFPOINT
            THEN WRITELN (CLASS [COUNTER].ID, CLASS [COUNTER].
            GPA)
   END.
```

12. We will assume that each line of the file is organized as follows: a name occupies the first 20 characters. It is followed by a GPA which is a real number, followed by the number of units (integer), followed by the number of years in college (integer).

```
PROGRAM CLASS (STUDENTS, OUTPUT);
{This program prints the name of the student with the
highest GPA.  Some restrictions apply}
TYPE
   TYPEOFSTUDENT = RECORD
                        NAME : PACKED ARRAY [1..20] OF CHAR;
                        GPA : REAL;
                        UNITS : INTEGER;
                        YEARS : INTEGER
                     END;
VAR
   STUDENTS : TEXT;
   CURRENTSTUDENT : TYPEOFSTUDENT;
   COUNTER : INTEGER;
   SCORE : REAL;
BEGIN
   RESET (STUDENTS);
   SCORE := -1;
   WITH CURRENTSTUDENT
   DO WHILE NOT EOF (STUDENTS)
      DO BEGIN
            FOR COUNTER := 1 TO 20
            DO READ (NAME [COUNTER]);
            READLN (GPA, UNITS, YEARS);
            IF (GPA > SCORE) AND ((UNITS > 30) AND (YEARS =
                                    4) OR (UNITS > 25) AND (
                                    YEARS = 3))
            THEN SCORE := GPA
         END; {of WHILE loop}
   IF SCORE >= 0
```

192

```
          THEN WRITELN ('THE HIGHEST GPA IS ',SCORE)
          ELSE WRITELN ('THERE ARE NO STUDENTS MEETING THE
                        CRITERIA')
    END. {of program}
```

VARIANT RECORDS

```
1. TYPE
       TYPEOFCATEGORY = (SAVING, CHECKING);
       STRING = PACKED ARRAY [1..30] OF CHAR;
       ACCOUNT = RECORD
                    NUMBER : INTEGER;
                    NAME : STRING;
                    CASE CATEGORY : TYPEOFCATEGORY

                    OF SAVING : (INTERESTRATE :
                    REAL); CHECKING : (PROTECTION,

                    ABOVE : BOOLEAN)
                 END;
```

2. The reserved word END does not terminate the variant part of a record definition. Rather, it terminates the entire record definition. Therefore, everything after the first END will be interpreted as the next definition, which is syntactically incorrect. Probably the intent of that definition was to introduce another fixed field, J, which should have been done before the variant part.

3. A record definition may include only one variant part.

4. The field identifiers must be unique throughout the entire record; however X appears twice.

5. The tag field type may not be real.

6. The constants (1 and 2) and the tag field (B) have different types.

7. The constant B appears twice.

8. The type of the tag field does not agree with the type of the constants.

9. a. The tag field is defined: it is B and its type is C.
   b. The tag field is not defined.
   c. This definition is invalid because no type identifier is given.

10. If PERSON1 is married and has dependents, assignments may proceed as follows:

```
PERSON1.NAME := 'JOHN SMITH';
PERSON1.AGE := 51;
PERSON1.MARSTATUS := MARRIED;
PERSON1.SPOUSENAME := 'MARY SMITH';
PERSON1.DEPENDENTS := TRUE;
PERSON1.NUMBER := 3
```

If PERSON1 is married but has no dependents, assignments may proceed as follows:

```
PERSON1.NAME := 'JOHN SMITH';
PERSON1.AGE := 51;
PERSON1.MARSTATUS := MARRIED;
PERSON1.SPOUSENAME := 'MARY SMITH';
PERSON1.DEPENDENTS := FALSE
```

If PERSON1 is separated, assignments may proceed as follows:

```
PERSON1.NAME := 'JOHN SMITH';
PERSON1.AGE := 51;
PERSON1.MARSTATUS := SEPARATED;
PERSON1.YEAR := 1981
```

If PERSON1 is single, assignments may proceed as follows:

```
PERSON1.NAME := 'JOHN SMITH';
PERSON1.AGE := 51;
PERSON1.MARSTATUS := SINGLE
```

11. Even though this record definition is syntactically valid, it is superfluous because there was no need to introduce the variant part to begin with.

12. This statement is invalid because the tag field is X and, therefore, the only valid variant fields are M and N. However, most implementations will fail to catch this error, which may lead to unexpected results.

13. Let us assume that we want to write the values of all fields of H. Then we can use this scheme:

```
WITH H
DO BEGIN
        .........
        CASE C OF
            X : WRITE (M, N);
```

```
            Y : WRITE (P, Q);
            Z :
        END {of CASE}
    END {of WITH}
```

14. We will assume that each line of the initial file is organized as follows: a name occupies the first 20 characters. It is followed by an ID (integer), followed by an M or an F for sex, followed by a salary (real). These are followed either by a U or an N for unionized or nonunionized employees, respectively, and if it is a U, the following 20 characters are a union name, but if it is an N, it is the last character of the line.

```
PROGRAM SPLIT (MIXED, UNIONIZED, NONUNIONIZED,
               OUTPUT);
{This program splits the file MIXED into two
files: one contains information about unionized
employees, the other contains information about
non-unionized employees}
TYPE
    TYPEOFCATEGORY = (U, N);
    SEXTYPE = (M, F);
    PERSON = RECORD
                NAME : PACKED ARRAY [1..20] OF
                        CHAR;
                ID : INTEGER;
                SEX : SEXTYPE;
                SALARY : REAL;
                CASE CATEGORY : TYPEOFCATEGORY OF
                    U : (UNIONNAME : PACKED ARRAY
                        [1..20] OF CHAR;
                    N : ()
            END;
VAR
    MIXED, UNIONIZED, NONUNIONIZED : TEXT;
    EMPLOYEE : PERSON;
    COUNTER : INTEGER;
BEGIN
RESET (MIXED);
REWRITE (UNIONIZED);
REWRITE (NONUNIONIZED);
WITH EMPLOYEE
DO WHILE NOT EOF (MIXED)
    DO BEGIN
        FOR COUNTER := 1 TO 20
        DO READ (MIXED, NAME [COUNTER]);
```

```
        READ (MIXED, ID, SEX, SALARY, CATEGORY);
        CASE CATEGORY OF
            'U' : FOR COUNTER := 1 TO 20
                    DO READLN (MIXED, UNIONNAME
                                [COUNTER]);
            'N' : READLN (MIXED)
        END; {of CASE}
        CASE CATEGORY OF
            'U' : WRITELN (UNIONIZED, NAME, ID,
                            UNIONNAME);
            'N' : WRITELN (NONUNIONIZED, NAME,
                            ID, SALARY)
        END {of CASE}
      END {of WHILE}
END. {of program}
```

7
Pointers and Their Applications: Solutions

THE NOTION OF A POINTER

1. a. In general the statement is incorrect although a pointer may, in principle, point to a variable of the pointer type.
   b. Correct.
   c. Incorrect: pointers can be neither read nor written.
   d. Incorrect: the value of a pointer can neither be incremented, nor decremented.

2. a. Incorrect: a pointer variable itself is a static variable.
   b. Incorrect.
   c. Correct.
   d. Incorrect. Even though dynamic variables are usually used to create linked structures, in principle, they may be used by themselves.

3. a. Generally, the statement is correct unless the variable has no external character representation. User declared ordinal variables are an example of such variables.
   b. Correct.
   c. Incorrect: the variable referenced by a pointer is anonymous. It can be referenced by using the pointer's name followed by an up-arrow or caret.
   d. The statement is incorrect.

4. The variable CHARPOINTER^ should have first been created with the standard procedure NEW.

5. The variable CHARPOINTER^ has been created but not initialized.

6. The values of pointer variables may not be used in arithmetic expressions.

7. The value NIL cannot be assigned to the variable referenced by a pointer.

8. The memory location BOOLEANPOINTER^ has been disposed of.

9. It is illegal to access the variable referenced by a pointer whose value is NIL.

10. The value of a pointer may not be assigned to another pointer referencing a variable of a different type.

11. The value of a pointer can neither be read nor written.

12. Only two operators are defined in Pascal to compare pointers: = and < >.

13. The pointer type should have been defined before the record type.

14. That is impossible. Pointers cannot point to static variables.

15. Yes, it may.

16. Yes, it may.

17. Yes, they are valid.

18. The former statement makes the pointer P point to the same dynamic variable that is referenced by the pointer Q. The latter statement assigns the value of one dynamic variable to the other.

19. Yes, they may.

20. Yes, it may.

21. No, the dynamic variable P^ has been lost.

22. The value of P^ at this point is undefined.

LINKED STRUCTURES

```
1. PROGRAM NUMBERS (SSNFILE, OUTPUT);
   {This program reads social security numbers from a file
    and creates a linked
```

```
   list of records containing these numbers}
TYPE
    STRING = PACKED ARRAY[1..11] OF CHAR;
    PERSONPOINTER = ^PERSON;
    PERSON = RECORD
                SSN : STRING;
                NEXT : PERSONPOINTER
             END;
VAR
    SSNFILE : TEXT;
    FIRST, CURRENT : PERSONPOINTER;
    COUNTER : INTEGER;
BEGIN
    FIRST := NIL;
    IF NOT EOF (SSNFILE)
        THEN BEGIN
                NEW (FIRST);
                FOR COUNTER := 1 TO 11
                DO READ (SSNFILE, FIRST^.SSN [COUNTER]);
                READLN (SSNFILE);
                CURRENT := FIRST;
                CURRENT^.NEXT := NIL;
                {See the first figure below}
                WHILE NOT EOF (SSNFILE)
                DO BEGIN
                {Now we can create and initialize next record;
                 see the second figure below}
                    NEW (CURRENT^.NEXT);
                    CURRENT := CURRENT^.NEXT;
                    CURRENT^.NEXT := NIL;
                    FOR COUNTER := 1 TO 11
                    DO READ (SSNFILE, CURRENT^.SSN
                            [COUNTER]);
                    READLN (SSNFILE)
                END
            END
END.
```

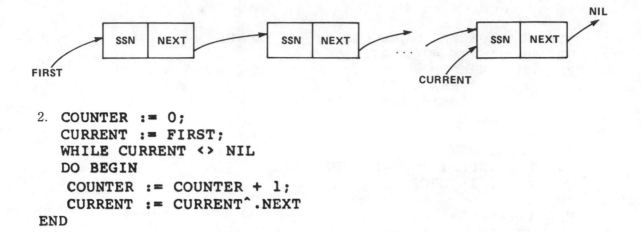

2. ```
   COUNTER := 0;
   CURRENT := FIRST;
   WHILE CURRENT <> NIL
   DO BEGIN
    COUNTER := COUNTER + 1;
    CURRENT := CURRENT^.NEXT
   END
   ```

3. Traverse the linked list to locate the right place and then reconnect the list.

4. ```
   THIRD := FIRST^.NEXT^.NEXT;
   FIRST^.NEXT^.NEXT := THIRD^.NEXT^.NEXT
   ```

   After the first statement the list looks like this:

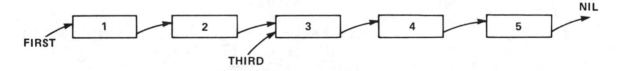

   The second statement makes the pointer field of the second record point to the fifth record:

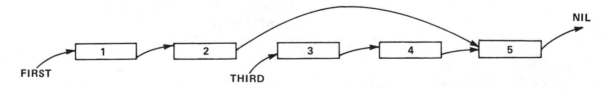

5. That can be accomplished with one statement:

   FIRST^.NEXT^.NEXT^.NEXT^.NEXT^.NEXT := FIRST

6. ```
   TEMPORARY := START^.NEXT^.NEXT^.NEXT;
   {The pointer TEMPORARY now points to the fourth node}
   TEMPORARY^.NEXT := START^.NEXT^.NEXT;
   {The fourth node now points to the third node}
   ```
   ```

```
TEMPORARY^.NEXT^.NEXT := START^.NEXT;
{The third node now points to the second}
TEMPORARY^.NEXT^.NEXT^.NEXT := START;
{The second node now points to the first}
TEMPORARY^.NEXT^.NEXT^.NEXT^.NEXT := NIL;
{NIL marks the end of the list}
START := TEMPORARY
{The pointer START now points to the fourth node}
```

Note that had we made the pointer START point to the fourth node in the beginning of the segment, the first node would have become inaccessible.

```
7. FOURTH^.NEXT^.NEXT := FIRST^.NEXT^.NEXT;
   FIRST^.NEXT^.NEXT := FOURTH^.NEXT;
   FOURTH^.NEXT := FIRST^.NEXT;
   FIRST^.NEXT := FOURTH
```

The sequential transformations undergone by the linked list are depicted in the following four figures.

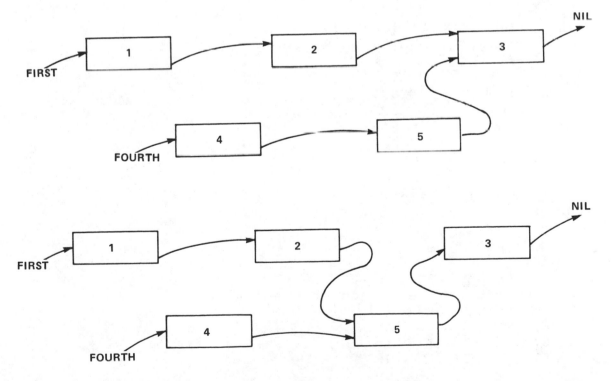

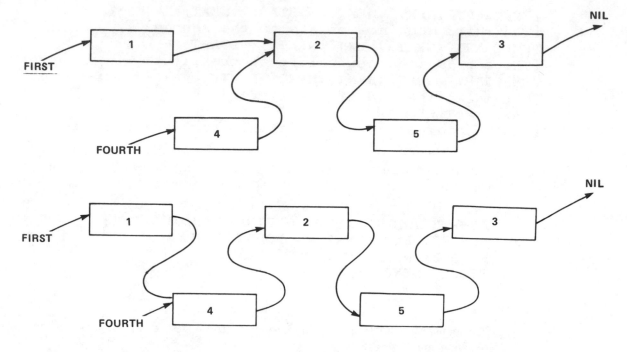

10. To make the program more straightforward we will not use a loop, even though a loop would make it shorter.

```
PROGRAM DOUBLE (OUTPUT);
{This program creates a doubly-linked list}
TYPE
    LINK = ^ENTITY;
    ENTITY = RECORD
                 INFO : CHAR;
                 P1 : LINK;
                 P2 : LINK
             END;
VAR
    FIRST, LAST : LINK;
BEGIN
    NEW (FIRST);
    NEW (FIRST^.P2);
    NEW (FIRST^.P2^.P2);
    NEW (FIRST^.P2^.P2^.P2);
    {All records have been created and we can initialize
     their INFO fields}
    FIRST^.INFO := 'A';
    FIRST^.P2^.INFO := 'B';
    FIRST^.P2^.P2^.INFO := 'C';
```

```
        FIRST^.P2^.P2^.P2^.INFO := 'D';
        {Now let us connect the links in the opposite direction}
        LAST := FIRST^.P2^.P2^.P2;
        LAST^.P1 := FIRST^.P2^.P2;
        LAST^.P1^.P1 := FIRST^.P2;
        LAST^.P1^.P1^.P1 := FIRST;
        LAST^.P2 := NIL;
        FIRST^.P1 := NIL
    END.


            11. PROGRAM TREE (OUTPUT);
                TYPE
                    STRING = PACKED ARRAY [1..10] OF CHAR;
                    LINK = ^PERSON;
                    PERSON = RECORD
                                NAME : STRING;
                                FATHER : LINK;
                                MOTHER : LINK
                            END;
                VAR
                    START : LINK;
                BEGIN
                    NEW (START);
                    NEW (START^.MOTHER);
                    NEW (START^.FATHER);
                    NEW (START^.MOTHER^.FATHER);
                    NEW (START^.FATHER^.FATHER);
                    START^.NAME := 'EUGENE    ';
                    START^.MOTHER^.NAME := 'SERAPHIMA ';
                    START^.FATHER^.NAME := 'BENJAMIN  ';
                    START^.MOTHER^.FATHER^.NAME := 'GREGORY   ';
                    START^.FATHER^.FATHER^.NAME := 'MOSES     ';
                    START^.MOTHER^.FATHER^.MOTHER := NIL;
                    START^.MOTHER^.FATHER^.FATHER := NIL;
                    START^.FATHER^.FATHER^.MOTHER := NIL;
                    START^.FATHER^.FATHER^.FATHER := NIL;
                    START^.MOTHER^.MOTHER := NIL;
                    START^.FATHER^.MOTHER := NIL
                END.
```

18 Style, Efficiency, and Common Errors: Solutions

1. IF <condition 1>
   THEN IF <condition 2>
           THEN <statement 1>
           ELSE <statement 2>

2. The program segment can be made more efficient by factoring out the common part.

```
SUM := 0.0;
COEFFICIENT := 2.7 * EXP (-3.1);
FOR COUNTER := FIRST TO LAST
DO SUM := SUM + COEFFICIENT * X [COUNTER]
```

or better yet

```
SUM := 0.0;
FOR COUNTER ·= FIRST TO LAST
DO SUM := SUM + X [COUNTER];
SUM := 2.7 * EXP (-3.1) * SUM
```

3. IF <condition 1> AND <condition 2>
   THEN <statement 1>
   ELSE <statement 2>

```
4. COUNTER := FIRST;
   WHILE <condition> AND (COUNTER <= LAST)
   DO BEGIN
         <statement 1>;
         COUNTER := COUNTER + 1
      END

5. FOR COUNTER := FIRST TO LAST
   DO <statement>
```

6. Standard Pascal leaves undefined what will happen if a subscript is not within its bounds specified in the array's type definition. Some implementations perform the run-time verification while others do not. Therefore, if a value greater than 30 is assigned to NUMBER, the program may overwrite some memory outside GRADES, which may lead to unexpected results.

It is a good idea to check the validity of input data in the program itself as follows:

```
WRITELN ('PLEASE, ENTER THE NUMBER OF GRADES');
READLN (NUMBER);
IF (NUMBER >= 1) AND (NUMBER <= 30)
   THEN FOR COUNTER := 1 TO NUMBER
         DO BEGIN
               WRITELN ('PLEASE, ENTER GRADE NUMBER ',
                        COUNTER);
         READLN (GRADES [COUNTER])
      END
ELSE BEGIN
      WRITELN ('THE NUMBER MUST BE BETWEEN 1 AND 30');
      WRITELN ('ENTER A NEW NUMBER');
      etc.
```

7. I is a real number. Its representation is machine dependent but may not be exact. These errors are compounded by real arithmetic, and there is no guarantee that the representation of I will ever be identical to that of 100.0. As a result, the WHILE loop can be indefinite.

There are two ways to correct the error. First, we can use a test for inequality that cannot fail:

```
SUM := 0.0;
I := 0.1;
WHILE I < 99.95
DO BEGIN
```

```
        SUM := SUM + I;
        I := I + 0.1
    END
```

The second way is to use a FOR loop:

```
SUM := 0.0;
I := 0.1;
FOR COUNTER := 1 TO 999
DO BEGIN
        SUM := SUM + I;
        I := I + 0.1
    END
```

8. b.

9. a. not correct
   b. not correct
   c. not correct
   d. correct
   e. not correct.

10. The statement implies that

   • A procedure should perform a clearly defined task that may occur in many programs.
   • If a procedure uses parameters and local declarations, it is independent of the other units and can be easily moved into different programs.

11. To get pseudorandom numbers uniformly distributed between 10 and 30, for example, multiply pseudorandom numbers uniformly distributed between 0 and 1 by 20 and add 10.

12. Generate pseudorandom numbers uniformly distributed between 0 and 1 and declare heads or tails depending on whether they are less than 0.5 or not.

13. Divide the interval between 0 and 1 into 6 equal subintervals and associate each face of the die with a subinterval.

14. The simplest program makes a move by determining a row and a column using two pseudorandom numbers. If the corresponding square is already occupied, it makes another attempt, and so on. A smarter program sees one move ahead. Namely, it should check to see if there is a winning move, or if there is a way to prevent the opponent from making a winning move.

15. I will assume that you know the formula for the area of a circle: pi * sqr (r) but

do not know the numerical value of pi. Generate a pair of pseudorandom numbers uniformly distributed between 0 and 1. Look upon them as a point on a square whose side is 1. If the distance between the point and the origin is less than 1, you can say that the point lies inside the unit circle. Keep tally of how many points are inside the circle. The area of a quarter of the unit circle can be approximated by the ratio of the number of such points to the total number of points. This will allow you to compute pi. Generally speaking, the number of trials determines the accuracy of the result.

20. See D. Knuth *The Art of Computer Programming*, v. 3, p. 159, Addison-Wesley, 1973.

19 VAX-11 Pascal: Solutions

1. No, it is not valid. The identifiers NUMBER__OF__PARTS and number__of__parts are identical in VAX-11 Pascal.

2. a. HELLO
   b. hello
   c. HELLO
   d. hello
   e. Hello
   f. HELLo

3. a. 82   c. 53   e. 63
   b. 114   d. 5   f. 43

4. In order to include a nonprinting character in a string, the string of printing characters is closed. The ordinal value of the nonprinting character enclosed in parentheses follows. Example:

   WRITELN ('X'(8)'__')

   will cause the character X to be printed and underlined. (CHR (8) is the backspace character).

5. PROGRAM MYSTERY ...
    .
    .
    .
```
BEGIN
    WRITELN ('HELLO');
    WRITELN ('WE ARE BEGINNING OUR PROGRAM NOW');
                .
                .
                .
    WRITELN ('GOOD-BYE');
    WRITELN ('IT WAS NICE WORKING WITH YOU')
END.
```

6. It is legal if the file XYZ.PAS does not contain further %INCLUDE directives. If it does, the construction may be illegal because there are restrictions on the number of nesting levels.

7. No, it is not.

8.
```
NUMBER := %b'0111 0011' DIV %b'1010'
NUMBER := %o'163' DIV %o'12'
NUMBER := %x'73' DIV %x'A'
```

9. a. It is $-(3 ** 2)$, or -9 rather than $(-3) ** 2$.
   b. Error.
   c. 1
   d. 0

10.
```
CASE A OF
    1:    X := 10;
    2:    X := 20;
    3:    X := 30;
    OTHERWISE
          X := 0;
          Y := 0;
END
```

11. Normally, the compiler does not generate code to verify that the value of a CASE expression is contained in a constant list, and the result is undefined. However, the programmer may specify the attribute CHECK as follows

```
[CHECK (CASE_SELECTORS)] PROGRAM ...
```

which instructs the compiler to generate such code. If so, in our example the system will terminate execution and issue an error message.

12. By default, the compiler generates code to verify that all subscripts are within the array bounds. If they are not, the system terminates execution and issues an error message. However, this capability can be suppressed if the CHECK attribute is specified with the following option:

```
[CHECK(NOBOUNDS)] PROGRAM ...
```

13. By default, the compiler does not generate code to verify that values assigned to subrange variables are within the declared bounds. However, the programmer can specify the attribute CHECK as follows:

```
[CHECK(SUBRANGE)] PROGRAM ...
```

which instructs the compiler to generate such code. If so, in our example the system will terminate execution and issue an error message.

14. There are two access methods:

```
MONTH [ 4 ] [ 2 ]
```

and

```
MONTH [ 4, 2 ]
```

15. That will cause a run time error unless bound checking is suppressed by specifying the CHECK attribute appropriately.

16. There are several solutions to the problem. First, if the current length of the string is not known, it can be obtained with the function LENGTH. In our example,

```
LENGTH (MONTH [ 4 ])
```

will return the integer value 5. Then the following statements will suffice:

```
FOR LETTER := LENGTH [ 4 ] + 1 TO 9
DO MONTH [ 4, LETTER ] := ' '
```

The same effect will be achieved by the PAD function. The PAD function has three arguments: the string, the fill character and the final length. In our case, the following statement can be used:

```
MONTH [ 4 ] := PAD (MONTH [ 4 ], ' ', 9)
```

Another approach is to use the concatenation operator.

17. It is convenient to use the SUBSTR function provided by VAX-11 Pascal. If the original length of MONTH [4] is stored in the integer variable OLDLENGTH, then the following statement can be used:

```
MONTH [ 4 ] := SUBSTR (MONTH [ 4 ], 1, OLDLENGTH)
```

where the arguments of the SUBSTR function indicate the source string, the starting position of the substring and its length.

18. It is convenient to use the INDEX function that searches for the first occurrence of a pattern in a string and returns an integer value equal to the position of the beginning of the pattern in the string. If the pattern is not found, the function returns 0.

Let the name of the string be LONG__STRING. Then the following segment will do the job:

```
PATTERN := 'MARK WEXLER';
NUMBER := INDEX (LONG_STRING, PATTERN);
IF NUMBER = 0

THEN WRITELN ('PATTERN NOT FOUND')
ELSE WRITELN (SUBSTR (LONG_STRING, NUMBER + 12,
                            11)
```

19.
```
START := CLOCK;
FOR ...
DO ...
FINISH := CLOCK;
ELAPSED_TIME := (FINISH - START) DIV 1000
```

20. No, a file can be opened with the RESET or REWRITE procedure. However, the OPEN procedure is more powerful than either RESET or REWRITE. It allows the programmer to specify a number of file parameters that otherwise take their default values.

21. The STATUS function called in program segment A tests whether the data was successfully read from the file FILE1. In program segment B it tests whether the file FILE1 was successfully positioned at the beginning of the next line.

22. In VAX-11 Pascal a string variable can be an argument of the READ procedure.

If the end of the line is encountered before each element is assigned a value, the remaining elements become blanks.

23. In VAX-11 Pascal Boolean variables can be both written and read. The default field width for Boolean values printed with the WRITE procedure is 6 characters. If you specify a field that is too narrow for a value, the value is truncated on the right. If a Boolean variable is an argument of the READ procedure, you need to provide only one character, T or F (in uppercase or lowercase), since they are sufficient to uniquely identify the value. However, any other abbreviated or full value may appear as well.

24. In VAX-11 Pascal they can be both written and read. The default field width for user-defined ordinal values printed with the WRITE procedure is the length of the longest value but no more than 32 characters. If you specify a field that is too narrow for a value, the value will be truncated on the right.

   If a user-defined ordinal variable is an argument of the READ procedure, you need input only as many characters as necessary to uniquely identify the values. For example, SP, SU, F and W can be used instead of SPRING, SUMMER, FALL and WINTER. However, longer abbreviated values and full values can be input as well. The values may be separated by any number of blanks, tabs, and end-of-lines. All characters of a value are read but no more than the first 31 characters are actually stored.

   Needless to say that this capability can simplify many problems.

20 TURBO
Pascal: Solutions

1. a, b, c, d, f and h are valid; e is invalid because it starts with a digit. g is invalid because it is a reserved word.

2. They are identical because TURBO Pascal is case insensitive.

3. They are distinct because they are less than 127 characters long and contain different characters.

4. c.

5. No. The first program segment will yield an unexpected result because of an undetected overflow.

6. a. **A := $64**
   b. **A := $1C7**
   c. **A := $D**

7. a. **A := 770**
   b. **A := 250**
   c. **A := 2862**

8. TURBO Pascal offers two ways of doing it:

```
1. WRITE ('HELLO'^H^H^H^H^H'_____')
2. WRITE ('HELLO'#08#08#08#08#08'_____')
```

9. Although that makes no difference, it is evaluated as $(-A) * B$ in TURBO Pascal. Note that in VAX-11 Pascal it is evaluated as $-(A * B)$.

10. $7FE9

11. 15

12. 5

13. FALSE

14.
```
CASE A OF
    1 : X := 10;
    2 : X := 20;
    3 : X := 30;
    ELSE
        X := 0;
        Y := 0;
END
```

15.
```
CASE SCORE OF
    1..4 : WRITELN ('YOU FLUNKED');
    5..7 : WRITELN ('YOU PASSED BUT IMPROVEMENT IS
                     NEEDED');
    8..10: WRITELN ('YOU PASSED')
END
```

16. a. FALSE
    b. TRUE
    c. TRUE
    d. TRUE

17. In the former case, all characters of the string starting with the 'O' will be loaded into the 2-nd, 3-rd, 4-th, . . ., 13-th bytes of the variable NAME. The first byte is always reserved for the current length of the string, which will be 12, and bytes 14 through 21 will be unused.

In the latter case, the last three characters, 'W', 'E' and 'R' will be truncated and the remaining part of the string, starting with the 'D', will be loaded into the 2-nd, 3-rd, . . ., 21-st bytes of the variable NAME. The first byte will contain 20.

18. A good (easily generalizable) solution to this problem is to convert NUMBER to

a string of characters and then manipulate individual characters of the string. The conversion can be accomplished by the standard procedure STR available in TURBO Pascal. Note that NUMBER cannot have more than five digits.

Assume that two string, STRING_BEFORE and STRING_AFTER, have been declared, even though one would be enough. The maximum number of characters in STRING_BEFORE is five. The maximum number of characters in STRING_AFTER is 10. SEPARATOR is a character variable. COUNTER is an integer variable.

```
SEPARATOR := ' ';
STR (NUMBER : 5, STRING_BEFORE);
FOR COUNTER := 1 TO 5
DO BEGIN
      STRING_AFTER [2 * COUNTER - 1] :=
            STRING_BEFORE [COUNTER];
      STRING_AFTER [2 * COUNTER] := SEPARATOR
   END;
WRITELN (STRING_AFTER)
```

19. The multiplication of string variables is not defined. It probably was intended to multiply 135 and 14 and assign the result to the integer variable C. This can be done by converting the contents of the strings A and B into integers and multiplying the results. The standard procedure VAL, available in TURBO Pascal, can accomplish the conversion. Let us assume that the integer variables AINTEGER, BINTEGER, CODE1, and CODE2 have been declared. Then here is a correct version of the program segment:

```
A := '135';
B := '14';
VAL (A, AINTEGER, CODE1);
VAL (B, BINTEGER, CODE2);
IF CODE1 <> 0 AND CODE2 <>0
    THEN C := AINTEGER * BINTEGER
    ELSE WRITELN ('ERROR WAS DETECTED BE VAL')
```

20. ALFRED TENNYSON

21. 0 because the string A does not contain the pattern PAC.

22. It is legal in TURBO Pascal but it would be illegal in standard Pascal. As you remember, constants in standard Pascal can be either integers, or reals, or characters, or strings. In TURBO Pascal, there are array constants, record constants and set constants as well.

23. It is convenient to use the POS function that searches for the first occurrence of

a pattern in a string and returns an integer value equal to the position of the beginning of the pattern in the string. Let the name of the string be LONG__STRING.
Then the following program segment will do the job:

```
PATTERN := 'MARK WEXLER';
NUMBER := POS (PATTERN, LONG_STRING);
IF NUMBER = 0
THEN WRITELN ('PATTERN NOT FOUND')
ELSE WRITELN (COPY (LONG_STRING, NUMBER + 12,10)
```

24. In TURBO Pascal a string variable can be an argument of the READ statement.
The READ statement reads the maximum number of characters used in the string
definition unless the end of the line or the end of the file is encountered before
each element is assigned a value.

25. TURBO Pascal does not provide for reading or writing of user-defined ordinal types.

26. It is valid in standard Pascal but not in TURBO Pascal.

Index

Edited by Marilyn L. Johnson